Handmade Heirlooms

Handmade Heirlooms

CRAFTING WITH INTENTION,
MAKING THINGS THAT MATTER, AND
CONNECTING TO FAMILY & TRADITION

Jennifer Casa

ROOST BOOKS

Boston & London

2015

Roost Books
An imprint of Shambhala Publications, Inc.
Horticultural Hall
300 Massachusetts Avenue
Boston, Massachusetts 02115
roostbooks.com

9 8 7 6 5 4 3 2 1

First Edition
Printed in the United States of America

∞ This edition is printed on acid-free paper that meets the
American National Standards Institute Z39.48 Standard.
♻ Shambhala Publications makes every effort to print on recycled paper.
For more information please visit www.shambhala.com.

Distributed in the United States by Penguin Random House LLC and in
Canada by Random House of Canada Ltd

Designed by Colleen Cole

Library of Congress Cataloging-in-Publication Data

Casa, Jennifer.
Handmade heirlooms: Crafting with intention, making things that
matter, and connecting to family and tradition /Jennifer Casa.
    pages   cm
Includes bibliographical references.
ISBN 978-1-61180-236-8 (pbk.: alk. paper)
1. Sewing. 2. Handicraft. I. Title.
TT705.C376 2015
646.2—dc23
2014034026

For posterity.

xoxo

Contents

What Do You Consider an Heirloom?

Think about a special keepsake that you have. One that was handed down to you. Even though you may have many, I invite you to give your full attention to just one for a little while. Simply close your eyes and think about it. What is it? A piece of jewelry? A book, perhaps? An article of clothing? A vintage tool or primitive machine? Maybe a patchwork quilt or a knit blanket? Now pause for a moment or two as you consider its relevance in your life.

How did you come to possess this heirloom? What was the occasion when you received it? Was it a gift made especially for you? Or is it something you inherited? What was the intention behind this piece making its way into your life? Why is it yours? Why do you care about it? And what do you intend to do with it? This is a lot to think about, to be sure. The act of meditating in this way—focusing on something that is special to you and honoring the path that brought it into your life—is an incredibly powerful gesture that enriches its significance in the present and long into the future.

By definition, an heirloom is an object of value that has belonged to a family for generations. Whether handmade or simply handed down, heirlooms have unique histories that are broadened by the lives they touch. They are mementos of days gone by that we get to relive and share with others. Perhaps yours is something simple, like a treasured wooden spoon that has been used to make "sauce" every Sunday for generations, knitting needles used to make socks for a loved one in the service, or a collection of souvenir spoons gathered over a lifetime of travels. My husband goes to work each morning at his family's Italian sausage-making business, an heirloom in the truest sense of the word, where he connects with traditions his father learned as a child working in corner stores of 1940s-era blue-collar Cleveland, Ohio. Treasured moments are preserved in our heirlooms, and they afford us the opportunity to reminisce and make connections that transcend generations.

Much like flipping through a photo album with others, the act of sharing heirlooms enriches these memories. During our first few months as parents, we received boxes and boxes of family heirlooms. Handed down to us were sweaters worn by my father as a baby, dolls and doll clothes from my mother-in-law, and even my first pair of shoes, all for our family to enjoy as well as for posterity. Newly handmade heirlooms were also added to our collection, including crocheted blankets and hand-knit sweaters created especially for our girls. A decade later, those thoughtful handmade gifts continue to be so special to us that I now carry on the tradition of making hats, booties, sweaters, and quilts for friends who are expecting.

Gifts made by hand have rich significance that goes beyond form and function. Whether created especially for someone or to commemorate a significant occasion, there is a story behind every one. Handmade heirlooms are made with intention; time, energy, and inspiration are all intertwined in the process of creating each one. If time allows, I prefer to make gifts whenever possible, putting my thoughts and love into each stitch during the process. As these pieces are shared over time, their significance and value are enriched by every life they touch. When something is handed down, so are stories about the original recipient and everyone else along the way, and yet another lovely stroke is added to a collective canvas of memories.

Everyday traditions and pastimes such as needlework permeate our daily lives and have become serendipitous heirlooms for many of us just as much as the keepsakes we hold in our hands. Sewing is a hobby my mother has shared with me throughout my lifetime, and at sixteen, I learned to knit from my host-mother while an exchange student in Germany. My daughters have come to recognize the familiar sounds of clicking needles and a whirring sewing machine as indicators that seasons are changing and new wearables are in the works. And as they have gotten older, they have begun to design and make their own clothes right beside me. Shared traditions like these continue to create a beautiful latticework of memories throughout our lives.

Food evokes feelings of nostalgia as well. Sharing a meal of heirloom recipes spotlights the joy, love, and pride in who we are. A dinner of roasted pork and mashed potatoes reminds me of childhood visits to my grandparents' lake house. When preparing our Thanksgiving table, I am sure to make pineapple cottage cheese salad for my father and maple-glazed sweet potatoes for my husband, because those are beloved traditions from their childhood. Family recipes, whether made to the letter or adapted over time, are a toast to our heritage. Our traditions are kept alive when we value special times like a shared meal.

Handmade Heirlooms is about the act of making and sharing memories. This book emphasizes the rich significance that heirlooms and traditions have in our personal histories, and recognizes the value in living one's life with intention. I hope you feel inspired to create all manner of things for the ones you love—treasures to be enjoyed now, and also handed down to future generations. The projects throughout this book are intended to cherish the value of handcrafted pieces, to spread the love of sharing handmade gifts, treasured recipes, and meaningful anecdotes with one another, and to celebrate special people and wonderful occasions throughout your lifetime. Your handmade heirlooms are an opportunity to give a bit of yourself to others, enriching their lives as well as your own. Sew, knit, craft, cook—share.

Needlework Notes + Handcrafting Supplies

To complete the projects throughout this book, you will need a familiarity with simple sewing, knitting, and crochet techniques. You will see common abbreviations as well as more specific terms with which you may or may not be familiar. Detailed explanations and tutorials can be found in the back of this book in the Stitch Guide (page 141) and Knitting and Crochet Abbreviations + Tutorials (page 143) sections. In addition, you may notice that I recommend pressing with an iron quite often. A pass with a hot iron will set the stitches and also streamline piecing and assembly. Ultimately, ironing is up to you, and I completely understand if it is just not your thing. That said, it is a really good idea to read through the instructions before embarking on any of the projects in this book. A thorough reading will give you an opportunity to get to know the plan and gather what you will need to have on hand. Take your time and enjoy yourself during the process of creating your own handmade heirlooms.

Following is a selection of tools and materials used throughout *Handmade Heirlooms.*

Ball Winder

This clever tool makes crafting easier for anyone who enjoys working with yarn. Often used in conjunction with a yarn swift, a ball winder transforms yarn from skeins and hanks into ready-to-use center-pull balls.

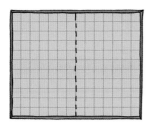

Blocking Board

This padded board features a measured grid and has a water-resistant lining so knitting, sewing, and craft projects can be wet-blocked with precision.

Craft Knife

Use this specialty handheld utility knife designed for crafting, drafting, and cutting with precision.

Embroidery Floss

Yarn that is spun specifically for needlework, such as embroidery, crewel, and cross-stitch, is called embroidery floss. Many types of threads are made from cotton, wool, or silk as well as synthetic fibers, and they are available in varying twists and numbers of strands.

Hook (Crochet)

This slender, dowel-like tool with a hook at one end is used to draw yarn through loops for crochet. Alphabetical and metric sizes on the hooks indicate the thickness of the shaft.

Hoop (Quilt + Embroidery)

Hold a foundation piece or quilt taut for even hand-stitching with this wooden or plastic hoop.

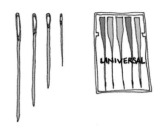

Needles (Knitting)

- Straight needles come in pairs and have a long rod that tapers to a pointed tip. A stop at the opposite end keeps the stitches on the needles while you are working.

- Circular needles (circs) are two straight needles connected by a flexible plastic wire. These are terrific for knitting in the round as well as straight knitting, and they work particularly well for larger projects because the connecting cable can drape and rest on your lap while you work without putting added pressure on your wrists.

- Double pointed needles (dpns) come in sets of four or five and are most commonly used to knit in the round for items such as socks, sleeves, and hats. Double pointed needles are thought to be the oldest type of knitting needles.

- For all knitting needles, US and metric sizes indicate the thickness of the shaft.

Needles (Sewing)

- Hand-sewing needles are available in many sizes. (If you can find vintage needle books with fresh needles inside, try using those needles when you hand sew delicate vintage fabrics.)

- Quilting needles have a sharp, tapered tip designed to go through the many layers of a quilt.

- Embroidery needles are slightly thicker with a wide eye and a light ballpoint.

- Universal sewing-machine needles are available in various sizes and sharpnesses for different uses. I recommend keeping on hand a few assortment packs of universal sewing-machine needles; these include several sizes to accommodate various thicknesses of fabrics.

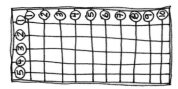

Quilter's Ruler

This clear plastic piece features a ruled grid, which is especially helpful for precise measuring, marking, and cutting.

Seam Ripper

Use this small, sharp tool to undo tight stitches without ruining all of your handwork.

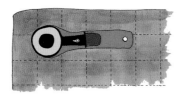

Rotary Cutter (+ Self-Healing Cutting Mat)

A rolling blade used with a specially designed, ruled mat, this tool is incredibly useful for cutting fabric into every shape and size imaginable.

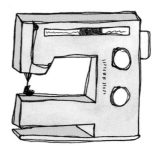

Sewing Machine

As long as you know your way around your machine, you are good to go—whether your sewing machine is as basic as it comes or fully computerized with hundreds of stitches and presser feet. Keep your machine's user manual nearby for quick reference if things go awry.

Scissors

It is a good idea to have a few different scissors on hand that are dedicated to specific uses, such as large scissors for cutting fabric, small scissors beside your machine for snipping threads, retractable travel scissors to keep in your knitting bag, and so on.

Single Hole Punch

This handheld tool is used to punch holes in paper and thin cardboard or plastic.

Stitch Holder

Knitters use this tool to hold "live" stitches when they are not being worked. In a pinch, scrap yarn also works well as a substitute for stitch holders.

Threads

A wide variety of cotton, silk, wool, and synthetic threads specifically designed for use with various needlework projects are readily available at craft and sewing stores.

Stitch Markers

Essential to those who knit and crochet, these little clips are used to mark the beginning of a round, indicate when to do a certain stitch, separate sections, and more. Think of them as knitting's answer to sticky notes.

Walking Foot

Surely my favorite sewing machine attachment, this presser foot is especially useful for machine-quilting and working with thick fabrics. It functions by synchronizing the top feed of layered fabrics through the machine in conjunction with the lower feed dogs, and it keeps everything aligned as you go.

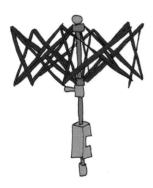

Swift (Yarn Swift)

This tool is used to hold steady and rotate a skein or hank of yarn while it is being wound into a ball. You can adjust its diameter so it will hold yarns of different sizes. (These can be pricey, but a swift and a ball winder are great investments for avid knitters and crocheters.)

Water-Soluble Pen

This tool is ideal for marking directly on fabrics for embroidery, quilting, and more because the ink disappears with a simple spritz of water.

Storing Heirlooms for Safekeeping

After having put so much effort into creating heirloom-quality pieces, you will want to be mindful to store them with exceptional care. Natural fibers, such as cotton and linen, need to breathe. Store them away from dust and out of direct sunlight when possible—if you have an armoire with glass doors, it will provide a protective environment while allowing you to admire them when not in use. Wool, however, should be kept in airtight containers in order to best protect it from pests. Lavender sachets tucked in among your woolens can provide additional protection against moths. A family trunk or cedar chest will provide a perfect environment for your heirlooms, combining history with your handwork in the name of posterity.

TO WELCOME

Future Generations

Children are our future, filled with hope for all that is possible. Their innocence and promise inspire us to connect and share with one another. A creative and nurturing environment allows them to flourish as they discover who they are. As a parent, I can attest to how incredibly heartwarming it is to receive gifts made especially for your child. In the first few hazy months at home with our twin daughters, friends and family shared countless handmade gifts in celebration of their birth and to welcome them to the world. Others thoughtfully prepared home-cooked meals that provided a delicious and greatly appreciated respite at day's end. The kind gestures of loved ones as well as strangers inspire me to carry on the tradition of making gifts by hand for the children in our lives.

Over time, traditional gifts such as bibs, blankets, and booties make way for more whimsical playthings. Just last year, we brought home the dollhouse my Grampa handcrafted for me as a child. It would have thrilled him to see how much our daughters enjoy playing with it every day and to know it is being treasured by yet another generation. Simple open-ended toys are my favorite to make and share with others. Children thrive when given the opportunity to craft their own stories

and let their imaginations lead the way. The process of creating handmade gifts for kids is tremendously gratifying, and as they are handed down, the story of each finished piece becomes enriched by many lifetimes.

Hiya Bib

Handmade bibs are a sweet welcome for new babies. Natural linen provides a simple, modern foundation for embroidering these timeless pieces. The linen fabric grows softer with each washing, and it has the added benefit of being incredibly durable and absorbent. This piece features simple quilting offset by a hand-embroidered greeting our family has said for as long as I can remember. Stitch up a few with words or phrases meaningful to the recipients so your creations will be used and treasured for generations.

FINISHED MEASUREMENTS
About 8½" wide × 11" high

NOTES

- Prewash fabrics to allow for shrinkage prior to cutting.

- Seam allowances are ¼" unless otherwise noted.

- Backstitch at the beginning and end unless otherwise noted.

- These bibs are fully reversible! Consider choosing a backing fabric that will be complemented by the quilted stitches you have planned for the piece. Smaller scale prints and polka dots work especially well to conceal baby's unavoidable drips and stains.

WHAT YOU NEED

Hiya Bib template
(see the Templates section, page 123)

Linen fabric for the front:
(1 piece) 12" × 12"

Cotton batting:
(1 piece) 12" × 12"

Cotton or linen fabric for the backing: (1 piece) 12" × 12" (see Note)

Water-soluble marking pen

Embroidery needle

Small embroidery hoop

Embroidery floss in complementary color

Thread in contrasting colors

⅝" sticky-back hook-and-loop coins (one pair)

Walking foot for your sewing machine (optional, but very helpful)

Free-motion quilting foot for your sewing machine (also optional, but superfun)

HOW TO MAKE

Prepare the
Fabrics

1. Press the fabrics and batting in half with right sides together. Place the template on the fold as indicated, and cut 1 piece each of the front fabric, batting, and backing fabric.

2. Use a water-soluble marking pen to write "Hiya" on the right side of the front bib piece, making sure that the word is positioned roughly 1" in from any edge. (Feel free to write another word, sketch a simple graphic, or perhaps write the baby's name in a lovely script.)

3. Place the front bib piece in an embroidery hoop, and embroider the writing by hand using a simple running stitch or backstitch or any embroidery stitch you fancy. When finished, spritz the stitches with water to dissolve the ink marks you made on the fabric. Allow it to dry, and then press the front bib piece on both sides.

Assembly

4. Place the back and front pieces on your work surface with their right sides together and then place the batting on top. Pin around all the edges. Sew around the entire perimeter of the bib, leaving a 3" opening for turning along the bottom edge. To reduce bulk, carefully clip the corners and inner curves, snip notches in the outer curves, and trim the batting to just beyond the edge of stitches.

5. Reach through the opening to turn the piece right side out so that the front and back fabrics are now right side out with the batting sandwiched in between. Use your finger or a chopstick to push out the corners and edges. Press the piece on both sides with an iron. Blind stitch the opening closed by hand.

6. (*Note: I highly recommend using a walking foot on your sewing machine from this point on. It will help to keep the top and bottom fabrics properly aligned while machine-stitching.*) Topstitch around the entire perimeter of the bib ⅛" from the edge.

7. Adhere the sticky-back hook-and-loop coins to corresponding points on the bib tabs so they will match up for wear. Secure them to the bib tabs by sewing an X across each one.

8. Free-hand draw a bubble shape around the embroidery on the bib front with the water-soluble marking pen. Switch to a free-motion foot to scribble-stitch around the writing several times. (*Note: If you do not have a free-motion foot, just work carefully using your regular machine foot or stitch by hand.*)

9. If you like, sew straight-line quilting in a grid pattern on the bib using contrasting-colored threads. Your lines need not be perfect; in fact, I rather like the organic look created by imperfect lines.

10. Wash the bib in warm water and tumble dry on medium heat to soften the fabrics and shrink up the batting just a bit, which will give it a well-loved, crinkly look.

Ankle Booties

One of the most charming items you can make for an expectant mother is a set of handcrafted baby booties. These soft little shoes are quick to knit with only one small seam to stitch when finished, making them an adorable last-minute knitted baby gift. They are sure to win the heart of the new mom while they keep her newborn's tiny toes cozy. Once outgrown, they can be saved for siblings and perhaps someday handed down to the next generation.

FINISHED SIZE
One size to fit ages 0 to 3 months

FINISHED MEASUREMENTS
3½" long × 3" high

NOTES

- This piece is knit flat with the soles seamed to the booties as you knit. When finished, there is only one small seam to stitch up the back of the bootie.

- W&t = wrap and turn. (See page 148 for a complete written explanation of how to complete this knitting technique.)

Yarn

100 yards of fingering weight wool or other natural fiber yarn (Samples shown were knit using less than 1 skein of *Koigu Painter's Palette Premium Merino (KPPPM) [100% merino wool; 170 yds / 50 g]* in color P715.)

Needles + Notions

US #3 / 3.25 mm straight needles (or size needed to obtain gauge)

One additional like-sized needle (for the 3-needle bind off)

Tapestry needle

Gauge

6 sts = 1" (2.5 cm) in Stockinette Stitch (adjust needle size for gauge if needed)

HOW TO MAKE

Cuff

CO 25 sts.

Work k1, p1 ribbing for 2".

Boot

Row 1 (RS): Sl 1, k11, m1, k1, m1, knit to the end of row—27 sts.

Row 2 and all WS rows: Sl 1, purl to the end of row.

Row 3: Sl 1, k12, m1, k1, m1, knit to the end of row—29 sts.

Row 5: Sl 1, k13, m1, k1, m1, knit to the end of row—31 sts.

Row 7: Sl 1, k14, m1, k1, m1, knit to the end of row—33 sts.

Row 9: Sl 1, k15, m1, k1, m1, knit to the end of row—35 sts.

Row 11: Sl 1, k16, m1, k1, m1, knit to the end of row—37 sts.

Row 13: Sl 1, k17, m1, k1, m1, knit to the end of row—39 sts.

Row 15: Sl 1, k18, m1, k1, m1, knit to the end of row—41 sts.

Row 17: Sl 1, k19, m1, k1, m1, knit to the end of row—43 sts.

Row 19: Sl 1, k20, m1, k1, m1, knit to the end of row—45 sts.

Row 21: Sl 1, k21, m1, k1, m1, knit to the end of row—47 sts.

Row 23: Sl 1, k22, m1, k1, m1, knit to the end of row—49 sts.

Short Rows
for the Toe

Row 24 (WS): Sl 1, p27, w&t.

Row 25: k7, w&t.

Row 26: k8, w&t.

Row 27: k9, w&t.

Row 28: k10, w&t.

Short Rows
to Create the
Seamless Sole

You will now knit these 10 sts in garter stitch to create the sole as follows. As you work back and forth, you will incorporate the wrapped stitch as well as one adjacent st from the boot into the 10th knit st in each row. This will seam the sole to the boot as you knit it.

Wyib, k9, sl the next st as well as the wrapped st purlwise to the right needle, use the tip of the left needle to pick up the wrap loop from around the last st, then slip it as well as the 2 previously slipped sts back to the left needle, k3tog, w&t.

Repeat this short row seaming method to create the base of the sole, working back and forth until 20 sts remain (10 sts on the center needle for the sole and 5 sts on each side).

Heel With RS facing, k10 across the center needle. Fold the work so that the 2 needles are parallel to one another with the RS of 5 sts (boot) and 5 sts (sole) together. Use an additional needle to complete a 3-needle BO across these 5 pairs of sts. Divide the remaining 10 sts across 2 needles, fold the piece RS together just as you did on the other side, and complete the 3-needle BO with these 5 pairs of sts.

Finishing Turn the boot inside out and use scrap yarn to stitch up the back seam to just below the ribbing. Weave in the ends, turn the piece right side out, and fold over the cuff 1".

Make a second bootie the same as the first.

Baby's Buntings

Colorful decorations draped across the front door are a welcome surprise when bringing a baby home from the hospital. Even though this bunting is made especially for the occasion, an heirloom bunting can be a special memento of a child's birth, and used over the years to celebrate a birthday, as charming room décor, or to eventually welcome the child home for visits from college and beyond. Whether you choose to sew a delicate garland made from vintage textiles or involve the whole family in crafting a colorful "welcome" banner, the good intentions that go into creating each heirloom bunting will become part of its history.

Sewn Bunting

FINISHED MEASUREMENTS
9'

NOTES

- Prewash and dry textiles prior to sewing. Delicate vintage pieces should be washed by hand.

- Consider resizing larger textiles. For example, as shown in the sample: doilies larger than 5" can simply be halved, decorative corners of luncheon or cocktail napkins can be trimmed off, and cutting the corners off of 12" handkerchiefs showcases their delicate edges.

- This type of bunting also looks quite lovely when hanging vertically. One of our daughters has several "snowflake garlands" made with different-sized doilies that hang down behind white window sheers, resulting in the look and feel of snowflakes year-round.

WHAT YOU NEED

A selection of small vintage textiles ranging in size from about 5" to 10", such as handkerchiefs, doilies, small dresser scarves, and embroidered luncheon napkins (see Notes)

¼"-wide ribbon: 3 yards

HOW TO MAKE

1. Have a look through your selection of textiles and arrange them in an order that is pleasing to you.

2. Place the ribbon on top of the arrangement of textiles, shifting them as needed. When you are pleased with the placement and alignment of each piece, pin the ribbon to the back side of each piece along the top edge.

3. Carefully bring the whole thing to your sewing machine and sew down the center of the ribbon, stitching it to each textile in the process. Backstitch at the beginning and end of each piece as you go, because those are the points where the ribbon will get the most wear.

4. Drape the bunting over a window frame or doorway, across the wall over a crib or bed, or anywhere that you like.

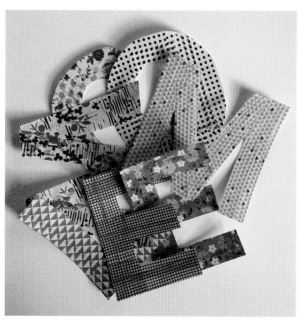

Crafted Bunting

FINISHED MEASUREMENTS
9'

NOTES

- Consider personalizing the bunting to include the baby's name.

- An alternative to decoupage would be to have the bunting professionally laminated at an office supply store.

HOW TO MAKE

1. Make a photocopy of template A.

2. Adhere strips of washi tape over each of the letters on the template in a design that is pleasing to you.

3. Turn over the template and use a craft knife and a self-healing mat (or fine scissors) to carefully cut out each of the letters. You should be able to see the outline of the letters on the back of your copied templates, but you can always work near a window or light to better illuminate the lines to cut, if needed. When all letters have been cut out, set them aside.

4. Trace template B onto the cardboard 7 times, and cut out 7 pieces.

5. Set out some newspaper to protect your work surface while painting. Place each of the cardboard bunting pieces printed side down, and brush acrylic paint on the reverse to cover each one entirely. Allow the paint to dry completely.

6. Glue each of the letters to a bunting piece, pressing well with your hands to smooth out any air bubbles. Allow the piece to dry, overnight if possible.

7. Apply a layer of decoupage medium over each piece to seal the letters. Allow the piece to dry completely and then repeat the application.

8. Use a single hole punch to make holes in the corners of each piece where indicated. Thread the bunting pieces onto the length of string through the holes in each piece, and hang it up to display.

WHAT YOU NEED

Baby's Bunting templates A + B (see the Templates section, pages 124 and 125)

Washi tape in an assortment of patterns and colors

Craft knife and a self-healing mat (or fine scissors)

Thin cardboard (about 4 cereal boxes measuring approximately 6" × 10" each)

A few sheets of newspaper

Acrylic craft paints

Paintbrushes

All-purpose glue

Decoupage medium (such as Mod Podge)

Single hole punch

String, yarn, or twine: 3 yards

Soft Serve Cap

Hand-knit head coverings for newborns are special treasures often handed down for generations. Knowing how much pieces such as these mean to our own family, I enjoy extending the tradition by gifting hand-knit items whenever friends and family announce the arrival of a new baby. Hats are incredibly gratifying to make because newborns will get a lot of wear out of them in their first few months, and they can be enjoyed by subsequent siblings, children, grandchildren, and so on. This sweet cap features swirls of knit and purl stitches that are worked in the round from the brim toward the crown. A charming dollop of I-Cord at the top completes the piece with a wink, creating a whimsical heirloom for the recipients.

FINISHED SIZES
One size to fit ages 0 to 6 months

FINISHED MEASUREMENTS
14" in circumference and 5½" from crown to brim

STITCH PATTERN
C2B = Cable 2 to the back (see Knitting and Crochet Abbreviations + Tutorials, page 145). This is a simple 2-stitch twist, made without using a cable needle, that borders the swirls of knit and purl stitches.

WHAT YOU NEED

Yarn

100 to 200 yards of worsted weight wool yarn (Samples shown were each knit using 1 skein of *Morehouse Merino 3-Strand Yarn [100% merino wool; 145 yds (133 m) / 2 oz]* in colors Natural White and Natural Chocolate.)

Needles + Notions

One set of four US #7 / 4.5 mm double pointed needles (or size needed to obtain gauge)

Stitch markers

Tapestry needle

Gauge

5⅛ sts = 1" (2.5 cm) in Stockinette Stitch (adjust needle size for gauge if needed)

NOTES

- To complete the C2B twist when working with double pointed needles, the instructions will occasionally necessitate shifting a single stitch from one needle to the next.

- It is simple to upsize this cap for older siblings or even adults by substituting bulkier yarn and larger needles. Do a bit of swatching and make adjustments to attain a gauge swatch of 3½ stitches per inch for a child and 3 stitches per inch for adults. I have even made one for myself!

HOW TO MAKE

Brim

CO 72 sts, and divide them evenly on 3 dpns (24 sts on each needle).

PM and join to work in the round, being careful not to twist sts.

Work k1, p1 ribbing for 1".

Hat Body

Round 1: [K10, C2B, p10, C2B] 3 times to complete the round.

Round 2: K9, C2B, [p10, C2B, k10, C2B] twice, p10, C2B, k1.

Round 3: K8, C2B, [p10, C2B, k10, C2B] twice, p10, C2B, k2.

Round 4: K7, C2B, [p10, C2B, k10, C2B] twice, p10, C2B, k3.

Round 5: K6, C2B, [p10, C2B, k10, C2B] twice, p10, C2B, k4.

Round 6: K5, C2B, [p10, C2B, k10, C2B] twice, p10, C2B, k5.

Round 7: K4, C2B, [p10, C2B, k10, C2B] twice, p10, C2B, k6.

Round 8: K3, C2B, [p10, C2B, k10, C2B] twice, p10, C2B, k7.

Round 9: K2, C2B, [p10, C2B, k10, C2B] twice, p10, C2B, k8.

Round 10: K1, C2B, [p10, C2B, k10, C2B] twice, p10, C2B, k9.

Round 11: [C2B, p10, C2B, k10] 3 times to complete the round.

Round 12: K1, [p10, C2B, k10, C2B] twice, p10, C2B, k10, C2B.
(*Note: In order to complete the C2B at the end of round 12, you will need to "borrow" the next st on the left needle. Be sure to shift the stitch marker afterward so it is properly positioned between the 2 sts of the C2B.*)

Round 13: P9, [C2B, k10, C2B] 3 times to complete the round.
(*Note: Only 71 sts were worked in this round because you already worked 1 st from this round as a part of the C2B at the end of round 12.*)

Round 14: P9, [C2B, k10, C2B, p10] twice, C2B, k10, C2B, p1.

Round 15: P8, [C2B, k10, C2B, p10] twice, C2B, k10, C2B, p2.

Round 16: P7, [C2B, k10, C2B, p10] twice, C2B, k10, C2B, p3.

Round 17: P6, [C2B, k10, C2B, p10] twice, C2B, k10, C2B, p4.

Round 18: P5, [C2B, k10, C2B, p10] twice, C2B, k10, C2B, p5.

Round 19: P4, [C2B, k10, C2B, p10] twice, C2B, k10, C2B, p6.

Round 20: P3, [C2B, k10, C2B, p10] twice, C2B, k10, C2B, p7.

Round 21: P2, [C2B, k10, C2B, p10] twice, C2B, k10, C2B, p8.

Round 22: P1, [C2B, k10, C2B, p10] twice, C2B, k10, C2B, p9.

Round 23: [C2B, k10, C2B, p10] 3 times to complete the round.

Round 24: K1, [k10, C2B, p10, C2B] twice, k10, C2B, p10, C2B.
(*Note: As with Round 12, in order to complete the C2B at the end of the round, you will need to "borrow" the next st on the left needle. Be sure to shift the stitch marker afterward so it is properly positioned between the 2 sts of the C2B.*)

Crown Decreases

Round 1: K7, k2tog, C2B, [p8, k2tog, C2B, k8, k2tog, C2B]*, repeat * once, p8, k2tog, C2B—66 sts. (*Note: This round actually starts with the 2nd st because the 1st st was used at the end of the last round.*)

Round 2: K6, k2tog, C2B, [p7, k2tog, C2B, k7, k2tog, C2B] twice, p7, k2tog, C2B, k1—60 sts.

Round 3: K4, k2tog, C2B, [p6, k2tog, C2B, k6, k2tog, C2B] twice, p6, k2tog, C2B, k2—54 sts.

Round 4: K2, k2tog, C2B, [p5, k2tog, C2B, k5, k2tog, C2B] twice, p5, k2tog, C2B, k3—48 sts.

Round 5: K2tog, C2B, [p4, k2tog, C2B, k4, k2tog, C2B] twice, p4, k2tog, C2B, k4—42 sts.

Round 6: C2B, [p3, k2tog, C2B, k3, k2tog, C2B] twice, p3, k2tog, C2B, k4. There is 1 st remaining to be worked: slip the 1st st from the next round onto the working needle and C2B those 2 sts. Be sure to shift the stitch marker afterward so it is properly positioned between the 2 sts of the C2B—36 sts.

Round 7: [P2, k2tog, C2B, k2, k2tog, C2B] 3 times to complete the round—30 sts. (*Note: As with round 1 of the crown decreases, round 7 begins with the 2nd st because the 1st st was actually used at the end of the last round.*)

Round 8: P1, k2tog, C2B, [k1, k2tog, C2B] 5 times and shift the last st to the next round—24 sts.

Round 9: [K2tog, C2B] 6 times to complete the round—19 sts.

Rounds 10–12: K2tog until 3 sts remain.

Finishing Work I-Cord (see page 146 for instructions) for 2". Cut yarn leaving an 8" tail and pull it through the remaining 3 sts to BO. Using the tail threaded through a tapestry needle, sew the tip of the I-Cord to its base to form a loop. Weave in ends.

Wet-block (if desired). To help the hat keep its shape while drying, you can inflate a small balloon, wrap it with a light towel, and place it inside the hat. You could also simply allow the hat to dry flat.

Anything + Everything Bag

Everyone likes a really great bag with lots of pockets to hold all sorts of stuff. Parents especially will appreciate this substantial patchwork bag with plenty of roomy pockets for baby gear and kid stuff as a great alternative to traditional diaper bags. It also transitions well beyond those years to be a terrific carry-all for the many functions they will attend with their children. Consider the recipient's personality and color preferences when selecting the four main fabrics for the patchwork, and anchor it with a sturdy fabric for the base. The high quality of your thoughtfully handcrafted work on this modern quilted bag guarantees it will be used and treasured for years and years.

FINISHED MEASUREMENTS

20" wide × 14" high × 6" deep

NOTES

- Prewash fabrics to allow for shrinkage prior to cutting.

- Seam allowances are ¼" unless otherwise noted.

- Backstitch at the beginning and end unless otherwise noted.

- You can make the entire lining of the bag with the same fabric, or use a contrasting fabric for the pockets as shown in the sample.

- The finished bag can and should be laundered as often as needed. Wash in cold/warm water and tumble dry on low heat. Over time, and with subsequent washings, the bag will take on a charming crinkly look reminiscent of an heirloom quilt.

WHAT YOU NEED

Coordinating quilting cottons for the exterior:
(4 pieces) 6" × 17"

Cotton canvas, denim, or heavier linen fabric for the straps and base:
(2 pieces) 5" × 30" and
(1 piece) 16" × 22½" from 1 yard

Lightweight natural fiber batting: (1 piece) 32" × 22½"

Cotton or linen fabric for the lining: (4 pieces) 16" × 22½" from 1½ yards (see Notes)

Water-soluble marking pen

Walking foot for your sewing machine (optional, but very helpful)

HOW TO MAKE

Straps

1. Press 1 of the 30" strap pieces in half lengthwise with the right side facing out. Use the crease as a guide to fold under both raw edges toward the center, bring the folded edges together, and press again. Topstitch the edges of both long sides. Repeat with the other strap piece.

Bag Exterior

2. Arrange the 4 quilting cottons for the exterior in rows. Match the long edges together in an order that you feel will work best for the patchwork. Sew the pieces in pairs with right sides together, pressing the seams open on the reverse and then pressing again on the right side. When finished, you should have one large piece of patchwork measuring about 17" × 22½".

3. Measure the center line across the patchwork (perpendicular to the seams), and cut it into 2 equal-size pieces measuring 8½" × 22½".

4. Place 1 patchwork piece and the base fabric with their right sides together. Align the fabrics along the long edge and sew them together. Press the seams to one side on the reverse and then press them again on the right side. Sew the other piece of patchwork to the other side of the base in the same way.

5. (*Note: I highly recommend using a walking foot on your sewing machine from this point on. It will help to keep the top and bottom fabrics properly aligned while machine-stitching.*) Pin and baste the batting to the reverse of the patchwork and base; then, machine quilt the right side of the bag directly to the batting. You can do this any way you like; I usually topstitch ⅛" from both sides of all seams and then add additional quilting such as simple lines across the base.

6. Fold the bag in half with right sides together and patchwork on top of patchwork; pin the sides together being careful to align the base seams. Sew both sides using a ⅜" seam allowance and press the seam open on the reverse.

7. Cut a 3" square out of both bottom corners of the bag. Open the bag and bring the cut edges on the bottom and side seams together,

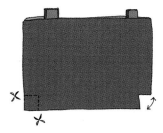

flattening the corner, and pin it in place. Repeat for the other corner. Stitch both bottom corners to create the boxed bottom for the bag.

8. Place the ends of 1 strap 5" in from each side seam, with the raw ends extending about 1" above top edge of the bag and the handle looping downward toward the bottom of the bag. Pin the strap ends in place, repeat for the other side, and then baste the handles to the bag ⅛" from the edge. Set the bag aside until the lining is done.

Lining 9. Fold 1 lining piece in half with the right side of the fabric facing out (so that it is still 22½" wide). Press along the crease with an iron and then topstitch ⅛" from the fold. Repeat with 1 more lining piece. (These will become the lining pockets.)

10. Place 1 lining pocket on top of the right side of a flat lining piece, aligning the raw edges along the sides and bottom. Place straight pins in a few spots to keep them together. Use a water-soluble marking pen to mark at least 2 vertical lines on the right side of the lining pocket (equally spaced or different widths—it is up to you). Topstitch the marked lines, which will create pocket nooks in the lining. Press both sides. Repeat for the other side of the lining.

11. Place the 2 lining pieces with the pockets facing together and pin the sides and the bottom. Sew the sides and bottom of the lining using a ½" seam allowance and leaving a 4" opening along the bottom edge for turning.

12. Repeat Step 7 to create a boxed bottom in the lining, but using a ½" seam allowance. Press all sides.

Assembly

13. Turn the lining right sides out and place it inside the bag (which should be wrong side out) so that their right sides are together and the straps are nestled in between. Align the side seams and pin the pieces together around the entire top edge. Sew the bag and lining together using a ½" seam allowance. Press the entire top seam to set the stitches.

14. Reach inside the bag through the opening in the lining to carefully turn it all right side out, gently pulling the straps out as well as the lining. Reach through the opening (to the inner workings of the bag) and push into the corners of both the exterior and the lining with your hand.

15. Pin closed the opening in the lining and then sew it shut.

16. Place the lining inside of the bag and press the top edge with an iron. Topstitch ¼" from the edge, securing the lining to the bag exterior along that top edge. (I like it when a little bit of the lining peeks up over the top.)

17. Carefully press the entire bag inside and out with an iron to set all the stitches.

Flying Ace Aircraft

New little ones in the house deserve special treasures to charm and delight their senses. These stuffed airplanes can float above the crib during baby's infancy and later be taken down to be enjoyed for years of creative play. Whether you sew or knit, the basic construction and clean lines of these airplanes are the same, resulting in an exceptionally soft toy to be enjoyed for years and years. This simple design allows children's imaginations to flourish and dream up countless flying stories to be shared each time these treasured toys are shared with others.

Sewn Aircraft

FINISHED MEASUREMENTS
10" nose to tail

NOTES

- Prewash fabrics to allow for shrinkage prior to cutting.
- Seam allowances are ¼" unless otherwise noted.
- Backstitch at the beginning and end unless otherwise noted.

HOW TO MAKE

Prepare the
Fabrics

1. Trace the templates and cut out the following:
   - 1 top piece A in main fabric
   - 1 top piece B in main fabric
   - 1 belly piece C in coordinating fabric, and 1 in heavy interfacing
   - 1 wing piece D in main fabric, 1 in coordinating fabric, and 1 in heavy interfacing
   - 1 wing piece E in main fabric, 1 in coordinating fabric, and 1 in heavy interfacing

2. Cut ¼" off all edges of the 3 interfacing pieces.

3. Center each of the interfacing pieces adhesive side down onto the reverse of each coordinating fabric piece (2 for wings D + E and 1 for belly C). Follow the manufacturer's instructions to adhere the interfacing to the fabrics.

Wings

4. Match the 2 wing pieces in the main fabric with their corresponding pieces in the coordinating fabric. Place the main fabric and coordinating fabric pieces with right sides together; pin. The interfacing should be facing out on the wrong side. Stitch fabric pieces together, leaving the short ends open for turning.

5. Clip the seam allowance of the wing tips to reduce bulk and then turn both wings right side out, gently pushing into the tips with your finger or a chopstick. The wings will not be stuffed; however, they remain firm because of the interfacing.

Airplane Body

6. Pin the 2 top main fabric pieces right sides together along the curved edge that runs down the top center of the airplane and the entire tail edge. Sew together along the pinned edge. Press the seam to one side on the reverse and then press again on the right side.

7. Pin each of the wing pieces to the airplane top piece about 3" down from the nose of the plane, making sure that the fabrics are right sides together. Baste each of the wings to the top piece ⅛" from the edge on each side.

8. Pin the belly piece to the main airplane piece with their right sides together (you will need to temporarily turn the aircraft inside out and nestle the wings inside). Stitch together the belly and top pieces, leaving a 4" opening behind one wing, which will be used later for turning and stuffing.

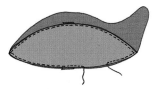

9. Carefully turn the airplane right side out, being sure to push into the tip of the tail and nose of the plane using your finger or a chopstick.

Finishing

10. Stuff the airplane with natural stuffing, gently pushing the stuffing down into the nose as well as up into the tail with a chopstick or your finger. Once your airplane is sufficiently stuffed, stitch the opening closed by hand.

Knit Aircraft

NOTES

- The knit airplane features Stockinette Stitch for the top surfaces and garter stitch underneath, giving a terrific dimension to the piece.

- This piece is knit in the round on double pointed needles beginning at the nose and working toward the tail, making allowances for the wings to be added after the plane body is complete.

- There is only a tiny bit of seaming to near the tail after the piece is stuffed, and then this plane will be airborne.

WHAT YOU NEED

Yarn

About 220 yards of sport weight yarn (Sample shown was knit using 1 skein of *Morehouse Merino 2-Ply Yarn [100% pure merino wool; 225 yds (205 m) / 2 oz]* in color Soft White.)

Needles + Notions

One set of four US #4 / 3.5 mm double pointed needles (or size needed to obtain gauge)

Stitch markers

Tapestry needle

Natural stuffing (such as wool, cotton, or bamboo)

Gauge

5 sts / 7 rows = 1" (2.5 cm) in Stockinette Stitch (adjust needle size for gauge if needed)

HOW TO MAKE

Cockpit CO 8 sts, and divide them over 3 dpns (3, 2, 3). PM and join to work in the round, being careful not to twist sts.

Round 1: Knit.

Round 2: (Needle 1) k1, m1, k1, p1; (needle 2) k1, m1, k1; (needle 3) k3—10 sts.

Round 3 and all odd numbered rounds: Knit sts on needles 1 and 2 (for the aircraft top), then purl sts on needle 3 (for the aircraft belly).

Round 4: K2, m1, k1, p1; k1, m1, k2; k1, m1, k1, m1, k1—14 sts.

Round 6: K3, m1, k1, p1; k1, m1, k3; k5—16 sts.

Round 8: K4, m1, k1, p1; k1, m1, k4; k1, m1, k3, m1, k1—20 sts.

Round 10: K5, m1, k1, p1; k1, m1, k5; k7—22 sts.

Round 12: K6, m1, k1, p1; k1, m1, k6; k7—24 sts.

Round 14: K7, m1, k1, p1; k1, m1, k7; k7—26 sts.

Round 16: K8, m1, k1, p1; k1, m1, k8; k1, m1, k5, m1, k1—30 sts.

Rounds 18 and 20: K10, p1; k10; k9.

Round 22: K9, m1, k1, p1; k1, m1, k9; k1, m1, k7, m1, k1—34 sts.

Rounds 24 and 26: K11, p1; k11; k11.

Round 28: K10, m1, k1, p1; k1, m1, k10; k11—36 sts.

Round 30: K12, p1; k12; k11.

Round 32: Repeat round 24.

Round 34: K11, m1, k1, p1; k1, m1, k11; k1, m1, k9, m1, k1—40 sts (14 on needle 1, 13 on needle 2, and 13 on needle 3).

Round 35: Repeat round 3.

Wing Spacers

Work 10 rows back and forth on needles 1 and 2 only as follows. Set aside the sts on needle 3.

Row 36 (RS): K13, p1; k13.

Row 37 (WS): Purl.

Repeat these 2 rows 4 more times, for a total of 10 rows and ending with a WS row.

Now knit 10 rows back and forth (garter stitch) on needle 3 only for the undercarriage section.

Midsection Decreases

Now begin working in the round again, starting with needle 1.

Round 46: K13, p1; k13; k13.

Round 47 and all odd numbered rounds: Knit sts on needles 1 and 2 (for the aircraft top), then purl sts on needle 3 (for the aircraft belly).

Round 48: K10, k2tog, k1, p1; k1, ssk, k10; k13—38 sts.

Round 50: K9, k2tog, k1, p1; k1, ssk, k9; k13—36 sts.

Round 52: K8, k2tog, k1, p1; k1, ssk, k8; k1, ssk, k7, k2tog, k1—32 sts.

Round 54: K10, p1; k10; k11.

Round 56: K7, k2tog, k1, p1; k1, ssk, k7; k11—30 sts.

Round 58: K9, p1; k9; k11.

Round 60: K9, p1; k9; k1, ssk, k5, k2tog, k1—28 sts.

Round 62: K6, k2tog, k1, p1; k1, ssk, k6; k9—26 sts.

Round 64: K8, p1; k8; k1, ssk, k3, k2tog, k1—24 sts.

Round 66: K8, p1; k8; k7.

Round 68: K8, p1; k8; k1, ssk, k1, k2tog, k1—22 sts.

Round 70: K5, k2tog, k1, p1; k1, ssk, k5; k5—20 sts.

Rounds 72 and 74: K7, p1; k7; k5.

Round 76: K4, k2tog, k1, p1; k1, ssk, k5; ssk, k1, k2tog—16 sts.

Tail Section

Round 78: K5, m1, k1, p1; k1, m1, k5; k3—18 sts.

Round 79: K6, m1, k1, p1; k1, m1, k6; p3—20 sts.

Round 80: K7, m1, k1, p1; k1, m1, k7; k3—22 sts.

Round 81: K8, m1, k1, p1; k1, m1, k8; p3—24 sts.

Round 82: K9, m1, k1, p1; k1, m1, k9; k3—26 sts.

Round 83: K10, m1, k1, p1; k1, m1, k10; sl 1, k2tog, psso—27 sts.

Round 84: k12, p1; k12; k1.

Round 85: Knit.

BO all sts.

Wings

Begin with the wing to the left when looking at the nose of the plane.

PU 12 sts along the top edge of the opening for the wing on 1 dpn, then PU 12 sts along the bottom edge of the same opening on a 2nd dpn—24 sts. PM and join to work in the round.

Round 1 and all odd numbered rounds: Knit.

Round 2: K9, k2tog, k1; p2tog, p10—22 sts.

Round 4: K8, k2tog, k1; p2tog, p9—20 sts.

Round 6: K7, k2tog, k1; p2tog, p8—18 sts.

Round 8: K6, k2tog, k1; p2tog, p7—16 sts.

Round 10: K1, m1, k4, k2tog, k1; p8.

Repeat rounds 10 and 11 four more times.

Round 20: K5, k2tog, k1; p2tog, p6—14 sts.

Round 22: K4, k2tog, k1; p2tog, p5—12 sts.

Round 24: K3, k2tog, k1; p2tog, p4—10 sts.

Hold the 2 needles parallel and do a 3-needle BO of these sts.

Now knit the wing that is to the right when looking at the nose of the plane.

PU 12 sts along the top edge of the opening for the wing on 1 dpn, then PU 12 sts along the bottom edge of the same opening on a 2nd dpn—24 sts. PM and join to work in the round.

Round 1 and all odd numbered rounds: Knit.

Round 2: K1, ssk, k9; p10, p2tog—22 sts.

Round 4: K1, ssk, k8; p9, p2tog—20 sts.

Round 6: K1, ssk, k7; p8, p2tog—18 sts.

Round 8: K1, ssk, k6; p7, p2tog—16 sts.

Round 10: K1, ssk, k4, m1, k1; p8.

Repeat rounds 10 and 11 four more times.

Round 20: K1, ssk, k5; p6, p2tog—14 sts.

Round 22: K1, ssk, k4; p5, p2tog—12 sts.

Round 24: K1, ssk, k3; p4, p2tog—10 sts.

Hold the 2 needles parallel and do a 3-needle BO of these sts.

Finishing
Weave in all ends. Stuff the airplane with wool stuffing through the tail section. Use a chopstick to gently push the stuffing down into the nose and wings. Once the flying ace is sufficiently stuffed, stitch the tail section closed by hand using scrap yarn and a tapestry needle.

Soft Toy Anymal

If the little ones in your life are anything like ours, they absolutely love their stuffed animals. Children's imaginations are broader and richer than any mass-produced toy manufacturer can anticipate, so why not let kids design their own stuffed pets. We call these "Anymals" because with a few minor adjustments to the template, you can create almost any adorable little critter. Be it a fox, mouse, kitty, or owl, these whimsical soft toys are so simple to make for (and with!) kids that you could create an entire menagerie in an afternoon.

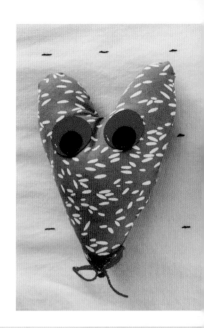

FINISHED MEASUREMENTS
About 7"

NOTES

- The process of creating these soft toys is the same, regardless of which template you choose. Consider also sketching out your own original template for an Anymal of your own design!

- Resize the templates to create bigger or smaller Anymals.

- Prewash fabrics to allow for shrinkage prior to cutting.

- Seam allowances are ¼" unless otherwise noted.

- Backstitch at the beginning and end unless otherwise noted.

WHAT YOU NEED

Anymal templates (see the Templates section, pages 128–130)

Cotton fabric for the body: 1 fat quarter yard

Felt scraps for appliqué

Natural stuffing (such as wool, cotton, or bamboo)

Yarn scraps for whiskers (optional)

HOW TO MAKE

1. Press the fabric in half with right sides together. Place the template on the fold as indicated. Trace the template onto your fabric twice, and cut out both pieces.

2. Cut out felt scraps for the eyes, nose, and other features. Pin these pieces to the right side of the front fabric piece and then topstitch ⅛" in from the edge. Press well.

3. Place the front and back pieces right sides together and pin around on all sides. Sew together around the entire perimeter, leaving a 3" opening for turning.

4. Iron both sides to set the stitches. Clip the corners and snip notches into any curves to reduce bulk. Turn right side out, carefully pushing into the corners. Press both sides again.

5. Fill the piece with stuffing, using a chopstick to nudge it into corners and tight spots.

6. Pin the opening closed and then stitch the opening closed by hand.

7. Sew yarn scraps through the nose area as whiskers, and knot the strands on both sides.

Ring Toss

An armful of these soft rings is an invitation to play any day of the year. They can easily be adapted into a myriad of games, the possibilities limited only by your imagination. Knit them using leftover wool yarns from other projects, adding to the collection over the years. You will be amazed by the variety of activities they are used for, be it dress up, ring toss, tic-tac-toe, hopscotch, or intertwined to create . . . well, I will leave it up to your imagination.

FINISHED MEASUREMENTS

Approximately 8" in circumference × ½" thick

NOTES

- To make larger (or smaller) rings, cast on more (or fewer) stitches.

- To make thicker (or thinner) rings, increase (or decrease) the number of rounds knit.

- For this project, you do not need to be concerned with gauge—really! The rings will initially be larger than expected, but the felting process will tighten the fibers into firm, densely woven rings with an incredibly soft feel.

HOW TO MAKE

CO 45 sts. Divide sts over 3 dpns and join to work in the round, being careful not to twist sts.

Knit 6 rounds.

BO all sts.

Repeat to make as many rings as you like.

Felt all of the rings (see Knitting and Crochet Abbreviations + Tutorials, page 145) and allow them to dry. Trim any stray strands of yarn.

NOW PLAY!

Toss the rings onto wall hooks or empty bottles lined up on the ground, or draw a simple target on the driveway using chalk.

WHAT YOU NEED

Yarn

Leftover bits of worsted weight yarns (The samples shown were made using oddballs of leftover yarns from sweaters and accessories I have made for my daughters over the years. See the Resources section, page 149, for a list of my favorite worsted weight yarns.)

Needles

One set of four US #7 / 4.5 mm double pointed needles

Wedding Soup

One of the kindest gestures you can offer friends with new babies is to bring them prepared meals during their first few weeks at home together. Something as simple as really good soup and a loaf of crusty bread will be greatly appreciated and allow them the freedom to spend more time getting to know their new family dynamic. Sharing a treasured heirloom recipe in this way is a kind embrace that will resonate throughout your circle of friends and family for years to come.

I make variations on traditional Italian wedding soup all year long that always possess the same key ingredients: broth, greens, pasta, and teeny tiny meatballs. Each time as I stand beside the bubbling pot, allowing meatball after tiny meatball to roll off my palm and into the pot, I am reminded of watching my late mother-in-law prepare this soup more times than I can count. The time involved in its preparation also allows me to think about the people for whom it is being made at any given moment. I have made this soup for friends with new babies and others going through chemo, for neighbors recovering from surgery, and, of course, for my own family on a regular basis. The pot is filled with well wishes for happiness and good health in addition to a well-rounded list of ingredients, and this soup is a home run every time.

Wedding Soup

INGREDIENTS

½ cup diced yellow onion

3 cloves garlic, minced

2 tablespoons olive oil or butter

1 to 2 cups additional vegetables to taste, such as diced carrots, celery, leeks, or tomatoes

3 quarts chicken stock

1½ to 2 pounds ground chuck (or ground turkey/chicken)

1 egg

Splash Worcestershire sauce

½ teaspoon coarse black pepper

1 cup Italian seasoned breadcrumbs

1 cup Romano cheese, grated, plus additional for garnish

1 cup uncooked tiny pasta (such as Acini de Pepe or Ditalini; see Note)

1 or 2 heads escarole (or spinach/chard), washed and cut into thin ribbons

PREPARATION

Sauté the onion and garlic in the olive oil or butter for a few minutes until they are soft. Broaden the flavor profile to suit the preferences of the recipients by throwing in extra vegetables at this time.

Pour in the chicken stock and bring it to a boil. Lower the heat, cover, and simmer for 30 minutes.

While the soup simmers, combine the ground meat, egg, Worcestershire, black pepper, breadcrumbs, and grated cheese in a separate bowl. Roll the mixture into tiny meatballs in the palms of your hands and drop them one by one into the simmering soup. Once all the meatballs are in, stir the soup every so often to ensure that the meatballs cook fully. Simmer for an additional 15 minutes.

Add the pasta and allow it to cook while the soup gently boils for an additional 10 minutes.

Drop the escarole ribbons into the soup and stir it until the greens are just barely wilted.

Serve the soup with freshly grated Romano on top and a slice of crusty bread on the side.

NOTE: If you are making this soup to package up and give to someone, prepare the pasta separately, rinse it well, and store it in a separate container. Deliver everything with a handwritten note instructing that the pasta is to be added when reheating the soup. Be sure to also include a loaf of crusty bread in your care package.

TO ENJOY

Everyday Traditions

Even those of us who do not consider ourselves a proper seamstress or skilled knitter can still create simple handmade heirlooms for the ones we love. Whether it is an annual tradition, something made to commemorate a special occasion, or something made simply because we take pleasure in the process, each of our creative souls can appreciate crafting a growing collection of handmade items to wear, play with, and enjoy throughout our homes.

In my folks' cedar chest are a few plaid wool Bermuda shorts that my mother wore in the 1950s and that I later wore in the 1980s. Their classic cut appealed to (and fit!) both of us during two entirely different eras. The cedar chest also stores cardigans knit by my grandmother that my mother and I have both worn. Her hobby has become mine, as have her knitting needles, which I inherited after she passed away. My own daughters will likely someday carry on the tradition of wearing those Bermuda shorts and sweaters, too. They will style them in their own way, to be sure, mixing in unique touches that will add yet another chapter to their story. Treasured heirlooms provide us with an undeniable connection to our past and allow us to bridge any perceived generation gaps with style. With a little bit of you in the stitches alongside the memories made while wearing them, making handmade heirlooms is a valuable tradition to keep up, as each piece is destined for the family chest to be enjoyed for generations to come.

Wool House Slippers

As family and friends enter your home, you want to welcome them into a space that is cozy and inviting. A set of thoughtfully handcrafted, soft wool house slippers is a great gift to share, or simply to have at-the-ready by your front door. Wool felt is naturally both warm and cool, making it the ideal material to use for slippers and comfortable in every season. These have become my absolute favorite studio shoes and my daughters' go-to house slippers. If you are feeling ambitious, an hour or two is all you would need to make a full set of these slippers for your kids and their buddies—or as the perfect hostess gift next time you are headed over to visit friends who have a no-shoe rule in their homes.

FINISHED SIZES
One size to fit ages 4 to 10

FINISHED MEASUREMENTS
9" long

NOTES

- I suggest making a muslin version of these slippers first to ensure a nice fit when done.

- Seam allowance is ¼" for this project unless otherwise noted.

- Resize the template to get the size you like.

- See the Resources section (page 149) for recommended sources for quality wool felt.

- To care for the finished slippers, hand wash in cool water and air dry. Machine washing and drying can cause further shrinkage of the wool felt and affect the sizing.

WHAT YOU NEED

Wool House Slippers templates for the Sole + Toe (see the Templates section, page 139)

3 mm thick wool felt for the soles: (1 piece) 9" × 18" (see Note)

Wool felt in a contrasting color for the insteps: (1 piece) 9" × 18" (see Note)

Straight pins

HOW TO MAKE

1. Copy and resize the templates (Sole and Toe), enlarging them as necessary to achieve your desired sizes. You will use the same templates when cutting out felt for the left and right feet, using the 3 mm thick wool felt for the sole and the traditional wool felt for the toe pieces. Trace and cut 1 toe piece and sole for the left foot, and then turn over the templates to the reverse and cut out 1 toe piece and sole for the right foot. Place pins in the felt pieces corresponding to the markings on the patterns.

2. Should you like to decorate your slippers, adding appliqué to or stenciling fabric paint on the felt works well. Incorporate those elements on the toe pieces prior to constructing the slippers. (*Note: Doing it at this point is much easier because you will work with a flat piece of felt rather than with a 3-dimensional finished piece.*)

3. Starting with both pieces of the left slipper right side up, place the toe piece on top of the sole and pin them together at the markings, aligning the edges of the felt. Continue pinning the top piece to the foot bed about every inch, ensuring that the edges are flush as you go. Being generous with the pins will ensure no hiccups while sewing.

4. Sew the toe piece to the sole, carefully finessing the felt to curve so that the edges remain aligned. Backstitch several times at the beginning and end of stitching when sewing the toe piece to the sole to strengthen the join.

5. Repeat Steps 3 and 4 for the right slipper.

Ashleigh Hat

Staying warm throughout the winter while expressing your own sense of style is all about confidence. This hat is named after my daughter's riding instructor, an amazing athlete and kindhearted woman with a lifetime of experience who has a wonderful talent for connecting with her students. Once temperatures drop below a certain digit, she wears an old-fashioned, fleece-lined hat, which seems to make her even more endearing. This hat is simple to make and customizable to suit the wearer's tastes. Whether worn with the earflaps tied on top or left to dangle over the ears, it is sure to become a signature piece for years and years.

FINISHED SIZES
One size to fit ages 5 through 12 (and many adults)

FINISHED MEASUREMENTS
24" in circumference

NOTES

- Prewash fabrics to allow for shrinkage prior to cutting.

- Seam allowances are ¼" unless otherwise noted.

- Backstitch at the beginning and end unless otherwise noted.

- This hat is fully reversible! Select a lining fabric, perhaps a whimsical fleece print, so the wearer can enjoy wearing this hat both ways.

- Be careful to note the manufacturer's recommendations for your chosen lining fabric. Most synthetic polar fleece should not be ironed, so you can skip that step with synthetic material.

WHAT YOU NEED

Ashleigh Hat templates A + B (see the Templates section, page 131)

Lightweight wool suitable for the main hat fabric: ½ yard

Flannel or fleece fabric in a coordinating color for the lining and straps: ½ yard (see Note)

Walking foot for your sewing machine (optional, but very helpful)

HOW TO MAKE

Prepare
the Fabrics

1. For the main hat and earflaps, use template A to cut 6 pieces each from the main fabric and lining—12 pieces total.

2. For the brim, use template B to cut 1 piece each from the main fabric and lining.

3. For the straps, cut 3 pieces from the lining fabric about ½" × 24".

Main Hat

4. Place 2 of the main fabric pieces right sides together, pin along 1 of the curved sides, and then stitch them together along that side only. Repeat with 2 other main fabric pieces. Press all seams open on the reverse and then press the seams again on the right side.

5. Now place those 2 stitched pieces right sides together and pin the long curved side, being careful to align the center seams at the crown. Stitch them together starting at the bottom of the cap going upward toward the crown and then back down the opposite curved edge. Press all seams on both sides and then set the piece aside.

6. Repeat Steps 4 and 5 using the lining fabrics, but use a ⅜" seam allowance and leave a 4" section open for turning along the middle of one side.

Straps

7. Knot together the 3 strips of fleece at one end. Braid the entire length of fleece and make a knot at the other end.

8. Mark the center of the braid. Stitch back and forth ½" from either side of the center mark. With the braid secured by the stitched lines, cut the braid into 2 pieces along the center mark.

Earflaps

9. Make a neat stack of the 4 remaining A pieces (2 in the main fabric and 2 in the lining). Cut 2" straight across the tip of all 4 pieces.

10. Place 1 main fabric piece right side up, then place 1 braid on top of it with the raw end extending beyond the top, then place 1 lining piece on top so that the right sides are together and the braid is sandwiched inside. Pin both sides and the short end and then stitch these pieces together along those 3 sides. Turn the earflap right side out and press well on both sides. Repeat this step to create the other earflap.

11. Topstitch the 3 seamed edges of each earflap ⅛" from the edge. Press well on both sides.

Brim

12. Pin the 2 brim pieces right sides together and then stitch along the curved edge.

13. Clip notches into the curve to reduce bulk when it is turned, being careful not to clip into the line of stitches. Turn the piece right side out and press well on both sides.

14. Topstitch the right side of the curved edge of the brim ⅛" from the edge. Press well on both sides.

Finishing

15. Turn the main hat piece wrong side out. Center the raw edge of the brim along the raw edge of one panel with the right sides together. Pin the brim in place.

16. Place 1 earflap inside the hat and center its raw edge along the raw edge of 1 panel with right sides together. (This should be one of the panels adjacent to the one with the brim.) Pin the earflap in place and then repeat this step to pin the other earflap to the panel on the other side of the brim.

17. Turn the hat lining right side out and then place it inside the main hat piece with all the other pieces nestled in between. Line up the seams and pin the pieces together around the entire circumference of the hat and lining.

18. Stitch the pinned edge of the hat using a ½" seam allowance. Press to set the stitches and then reach through the opening in the lining and turn the entire hat right side out.

19. Pin closed the opening and then stitch it together. Place the lining inside the hat and press it well, inside and out.

20. Topstitch on the right side around the entire base of the hat ⅛" from the edge. Press well one final time.

21. Turn the brim up against the hat so that the lining shows when worn or leave down as a visor.

Ombré Dot Leg Warmers

I just love leg warmers, especially for kids. Not only do they provide that extra layer of warmth for their little legs, but they also are such a cute way to express one's style—at any age. These are knit using two strands of yarn on thick needles, adjusting the combination of colors repeatedly to give a gradient effect that flares gently at the ankle. When outgrown, these leg warmers can be worn on the wrists as yet another stylish accessory for all ages.

FINISHED SIZES
One size to fit ages 3 to 8

FINISHED MEASUREMENTS
Approximately 11" around × 13" tall

STITCH PATTERN

Dot Stitch

Round 1: Knit.

Round 2: * (K3, p1), repeat from * for entire round.

Round 3: Knit.

Round 4: K1, * (p1, k3), repeat from * until 3 sts remain, p1, k2.

WHAT YOU NEED

Yarn

100 yards each of 3 colors of worsted weight wool yarn (Sample shown was knit using 3 skeins total of *Quince & Co. Lark [100% American wool; 134 yds (123 m) / 50 g]* in colors Glacier, Bird's Egg, and Fjord.)

Needles + Notions

One set of four US #10.5 / 6.5 mm double pointed needles (or size needed to obtain gauge)

Stitch markers

Tapestry needle

Gauge

3 sts / 4 rows = 1" (2.5 cm) using 2 strands of yarn in Dot Stitch Pattern (adjust needle size for gauge as needed)

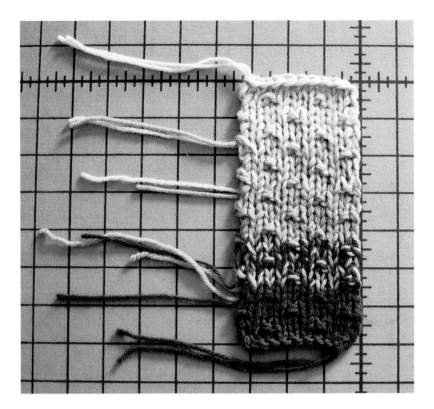

NOTES

- Determine the order of your three chosen yarn colors, remembering that the tones will intermingle when strands are combined. I like the appearance of lightly saturated hues seeping into a more heavily saturated tone in the same color family.

- In the directions that follow, the color at the cast-on edge (the knee) will be referred to as A, the color in the middle as B, and the color at the ankle as C.

- You will be working in Dot Stitch (see Stitch Pattern on page 65), a 4-round sequence, from the ribbing all the way to the BO edge at the ankle. You will change colors along the way, either on round 1 or round 3. (Changing yarn colors on odd numbered rounds makes for smooth color transitions.)

HOW TO MAKE

CO 32 sts using 2 strands of Yarn A, and divide the sts evenly over 3 dpns. PM and join to work in the round, being careful not to twist sts.

Work k1, p1 ribbing for 8 rounds.

Begin the next round using 1 strand each of Yarns A + B.

Work 6 rounds of Dot Stitch, ending with round 2.

Begin the next round using 2 strands of Yarn B.

Work 8 rounds of Dot Stitch, starting with round 3 in the pattern and ending with round 2.

Begin the next round using 1 strand each of Yarns B + C.

Work 10 rounds of Dot Stitch, starting with round 3 and ending with round 4.

Begin the next round using 2 strands of Yarn C.

Work 12 rounds of Dot Stitch, starting with round 1 and ending with round 4.

BO all sts and weave in ends.

Work the second leg warmer the same as the first.

Easy-Going Mittens

A new pair of birthday mittens is
a sweet tradition we have settled into
in recent years. What with our daughters'
special day falling right in the midst of the winter
holiday whirlwind when time is tight, I am drawn to making
quick and cozy accessories especially for each of them to use and
enjoy all winter long. These mittens are simple to sew and knit, made to
last, and a wonderfully sentimental gesture to share with the ones you love.

Knit Mittens

FINISHED SIZES
Small/Toddler (Medium/Big Kid, Large/Adult)

FINISHED MEASUREMENTS
5" (6", 7") wrist circumference ×
5" (8", 9") cuff to fingertips

NOTES

- These mittens are knit flat in one piece with one quick seam to sew afterward.

- Shaping for the tops of the mittens is done one side at a time.

- The Large/Adult size requires about 150 yards of yarn for the pair, which is more than the yarn I used for the samples has per skein. When I realized that a bit more yardage was needed, I opted to knit the fingertips with contrasting-colored yarn I had on hand leftover from making the Medium/Big Kid size samples. This was done simply by switching to CC yarn at the Top Shaping portion of the pattern. (This was really a happy accident because I really like the finished look of the dipped fingertips.)

- An alternative finish would be to stitch the seam with wrong sides together, using decorative cross-stitching in contrasting-colored yarn.

Yarn

134 yards of worsted weight wool yarn (Samples shown were each knit using 1 skein of *Quince & Co. Lark [100% American wool; 134 yds (123 m) / 50 g]* in colors Split Pea [S], Goldfinch [M], and Petal [L]. See Note.)

Needles + Notions

US #5 / 3.75 mm straight needles

Stitch holder

Tapestry needles

Gauge

5 sts / 7 rows = 1" (2.5 cm) in Stockinette Stitch

HOW TO MAKE

Cuff

CO 30 (34, 40) sts.

Work k1, p1 rib for 12 (14, 16) rows.

Thumb Shaping

Next row (RS): K1, m1, knit to the last st, m1, k1—32 (36, 42) sts.

Next row (WS): Sl 1, purl to the end of row.

Repeat these 2 rows 5 (7, 9) more times—42 (50, 60) sts.

Thumb Shaping Right Side

Row 1: Sl 1, m1, k3 (5, 7), k2tog. Turn work.

Row 2: Sl 1, p5 (7, 9).

Row 3: K2tog tbl, k2 (4, 6), k2tog—4 (6, 8) sts. Turn work.

Row 4: Sl 1, p3 (5, 7).

Small size, skip ahead to **.

Row 5: K2tog tbl, k2 (4), k2tog—4 (6) sts.

Row 6: Sl 1, p3 (5).

Medium size, skip ahead to **.

Row 7: K2tog tbl, k4, k2tog—6 sts.

Row 8: Sl 1, p5.

Row 9: K2tog tbl, k2, k2tog—4 sts.

Row 10: Sl 1, p3.

**All Sizes

Next row (RS): K2tog tbl, k2tog. Turn work.

Next row (WS): P2tog, cut a 3" tail of yarn and pull it through the loop.

Thumb Shaping Left Side

With RS facing, sl 30 (34, 40) sts from the left needle onto a stitch holder.

Row 1: K2tog tbl, k3 (5, 7), m1, k1.

Row 2: Sl 1, p5 (7, 9). Turn work.

Repeat these instructions to complete the left-side thumb shaping starting with Row 3 and working through BO according to small (medium, large) sizes.

Palm

With RS facing, slip the 30 (34, 40) sts from the stitch holder back onto the left needle.

Work St st for 6 (16, 16) rows.

Top Shaping

Top Shaping Right Side

Row 1: Sl 1, k2tog tbl, k9 (11, 14), k2tog, k1. Turn work.

Row 2: Sl 1, p12 (14, 17).

Row 3: Sl 1, k2tog tbl, k7 (9, 12), k2tog, k1. Turn work.

Row 4: Sl 1, p10 (12, 15).

Row 5: Sl 1, k2tog tbl, k5 (7, 10), k2tog, k1. Turn work.

Row 6: Sl 1, p8 (10, 13).

Small Size

BO these 9 sts and repeat for the other side to work the same top shaping rows (according to size) for the top left part of the mitten.

Medium Size

Repeat rows 5 and 6 as for the small size, then BO 11 and repeat for the other side to work the same top shaping rows (according to size) for the top left part of the mitten.

Large Size

Row 7: Sl 1, k2tog tbl, k8, k2tog, k1. Turn work.

Row 8: Sl 1, p 11.

Row 9: Sl 1, k2tog tbl, k6, k2tog, k1. Turn work.

Row 10: Sl 1, p 9.

BO these 10 sts and repeat for the other side to work the same top shaping rows (according to size) for the top left part of the mitten.

Make a second mitten the same as the first.

Finishing

Block both mittens flat. Weave in all ends.

Working 1 mitten at a time, fold the mitten WS together. Use coordinating yarn and a tapestry needle to seam together the mitten, aligning the edges from ribbed cuff along the thumbs and over the curved top. Repeat for the other mitten, and weave in the last few ends.

Sewn Mittens

Small/Toddler (Medium/Big Kid, Large/Adult)

FINISHED MEASUREMENTS
6" (8½", 10") wrist circumference when stretched
× 7" (8½", 9½") cuff to fingertips

NOTES

- Prewash fabrics to allow for shrinkage prior
  to cutting.

- Most synthetic polar fleece should not be ironed. Be
  careful to note the manufacturer's recommendations
  for your chosen fabric.

- Seam allowances are ¼" unless otherwise noted.

- Backstitch at the beginning and end unless
  otherwise noted.

WHAT YOU NEED

Easy-Going Mittens templates
(see the Templates section,
pages 133–135)

Fleece or wool fabric: ½ yard
(see Note)

½"-wide elastic: 18" (22", 26")

Walking foot for your sewing
machine (optional, but very
helpful)

Embroidery floss and needle
(optional)

HOW TO MAKE

1. Trace the template corresponding to the desired size, and cut 2 pieces of your mitten fabric.

2. If you are using polar fleece, you can leave the cuff edge raw, as shown in the samples. If you are using wool or thick flannel, you may wish to hem the cuff. To do this, fold the edge under ¼" twice and then topstitch on the right side slightly less than ¼" in from the edge.

3. Cut 2 pieces of elastic measuring 4½" (5½", 6½"). Pin the elastic at the center and sides as indicated on the template. Stretch the elastic so that it fits the fabric while sewing it in place using a zigzag stitch.

4. Fold the mitten right sides together and pin the entire side edge. Sew the mitten together.

5. Make a second mitten the same as the first.

6. Turn both mittens right side out, and they are ready to wear immediately. Add embroidery stitches to the seam for added detail, if you like.

Popover Tunic

When you spend the time and energy to make handmade garments, especially those for children, I recommend creating something special that can last more than a few months before it is outgrown. I designed this piece to fit toddler girls as a sweet dress and then become a top to wear well into the school years. Whether worn with bare shoulders in the summertime or layered over long sleeves in colder months, this charming top has classic style that will ensure it is loved for generations.

FINISHED SIZES
One size to fit ages 2 to 8

FINISHED MEASUREMENTS
About 24" around at the chest and
14" from neck to hem

NOTES

- Prewash fabrics to allow for shrinkage prior to cutting.

- Seam allowances are ¼" unless otherwise noted.

- Backstitch at the beginning and end unless otherwise noted.

HOW TO MAKE

1. Trace the template onto the fabric and cut 2 pieces: 1 for the front and 1 for the back.

2. Measure and cut 1 piece of fabric 13" × 36" for the bottom edge of the tunic.

Popover Tunic template
(see the Templates section,
page 132)

Cotton or linen fabric: ½ yard

Hand-sewing needle and thread

¾"-wide double-fold fabric binding (either made from a coordinating fabric, or prepackaged double-fold bias binding): 3 yards

3. Use a needle and thread to hand sew a straight running stitch ¼" down from the raw edge and across the top edge of the bottom fabric piece. Leave a 10" tail of thread at both ends of the line of stitches, and do not backstitch at the beginning and end. Gently pull the thread on 1 side to create gathers. Nudge the gathers evenly across the fabric. Repeat the pulling and gathering on the other side. Even out the gathers across the width of the fabric so that it measures 26" wide.

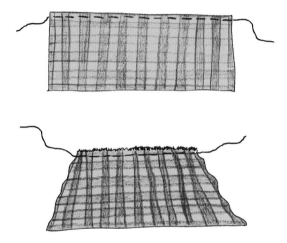

4. Machine stitch the top edge of the gathered fabric piece.

5. Place the bottom fabric piece right side up on your work surface. Place one top piece right side down on top of it, and starting 1" in from one side, pin it in place. Repeat this step with the other top piece. Stitch the top pieces to the bottom piece using a ⅜" seam allowance. Use an overlock stitch (or serger) across this edge one final time to keep the edges from fraying. Press both sides.

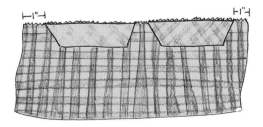

HANDMADE HEIRLOOMS

6. Align the 2 sides of the tunic with right sides together, and pin along the open side. Sew the side seam from top to bottom and then secure the raw edges using an overlock stitch (or serger) or zigzag stitch to keep the edges from fraying. Press both sides.

7. Cut an 8" piece of double-fold fabric binding and pin it over the top raw edge of the neckline. Stitch the binding in place ⅛" in from the bottom edge of the binding. Press and trim the excess. Repeat for the other neckline edge.

8. Cut a 1-yard piece of fabric binding for 1 strap. Align the center of the fabric binding with the center of the underarm and pin it in place along the edges of the arm opening on the front and back. (The straps tie at the shoulder. Each strap runs from the front shoulder, down the front of the arm opening, under the arm, and up the back of the arm opening to the back shoulder.) Start at one end of the fabric binding and then work the entire length of it to stitch ⅛" in from the open edge. Press and make a knot at both ends of the fabric binding or stitch the ends closed. Repeat this step for the other strap.

9. Fold over the bottom hem ¼" and press. Fold it over again and press again. Topstitch the hem a scant ¼" in from the edge. Press the entire piece.

10. Tie the straps at the shoulders to fit to the wearer.

Take-Along Sewing Kit

For many of us, needlework has surpassed hobby status. We all know someone who sews pretty much every day. For so many, sewing is a recreational activity that extends into every facet of their lives. Be it working on quilts for people in need, personal projects that seem to take forever (like the Dear Jane quilt my mother has been stitching for years), or smaller projects like bags and such, sewing can be a steadfast companion that gets you through rough times by focusing your energy on the creation of something positive.

When I first shared the proposal for this book with my agent, Linda, she reminisced about a needle book she inherited from her Aunt Theresa. That piece continues to mean a great deal to her as a reminder of their special connection, most notably their shared love of books and needlework. Their story inspired this simple travel sewing kit. It can be made quickly using materials you already have on hand, which is part of its charm. There is a little pincushion that doubles as a pocket for threads, a few soft felt pages for needles, and even a handy scissors sleeve in the back. I hope that Linda will enjoy making this piece as much as she will use it, in the same way as I imagine her Aunt Theresa would have. Make one, use and enjoy it, and then someday hand it down to someone special who shares your love of needlework.

FINISHED MEASUREMENTS
5" × 5"

NOTES

- Use pinking shears to cut a zigzag edge on all sides of the fabric squares to prevent fraying.

- Seam allowances are ¼" unless otherwise noted.

- Backstitch at the beginning and end unless otherwise noted.

WHAT YOU NEED

An assortment of fabric (charm squares are great for this): (5 pieces) 5" square

Natural fiber quilt batting: (2 pieces) 4½" square

Thin ribbon for the ties: (2 pieces) 5"

Thick wool felt, canvas, denim, or even leather for the scissors sleeve: (1 piece) 3" square

Wool felt or flannel for needle storage: (2 pieces) 4" × 4½"

A small handful of wool stuffing or polyfill

Walking foot for your sewing machine (optional, but very helpful)

HOW TO MAKE

1. Place 1 square of fabric right side down on your work surface. Center 1 batting square on it, then place a 2nd fabric square right side up on top. Slip 1 ribbon inside the fabric sandwich by about ½" and center it on 1 side; then, pin everything together. Sew around all 4 sides ¼" from the edge. This will be the front of the sewing kit. Repeat to create another piece just like this one, ribbon and all, which will be used as the back piece.

2. Now set a small pair of scissors on top of the scrap fabric you are using for the scissors sleeve. Trace a triangle around the point and up to just below the grip and then add an additional ⅓" around the actual shape of the scissors. Cut out the fabric and pin it to what will be the inside back of the sewing kit. Play around with the positioning of the scissors before you pin to ensure that it will fit the scissors. Sew the fabric for the scissors sleeve directly to the inside of the back piece. Set this piece aside.

3. Fold the 1 remaining fabric square in half with the right side out, and press along the fold. Position the folded fabric vertically on the inside front piece with the fold down the center and the raw edges aligned at the left. Pin the top, bottom, and left sides; then, sew those 3 sides ¼" from the edge but leave a 2" opening at the side so you can fill it with stuffing to make a pincushion. Once sufficiently stuffed, pin and sew the opening together.

4. Place the back piece right side up, center the 2 felt pieces for needles on top of it, aligning their edges at the left, and then place the front piece on top, cushion side down. Pin the left edge, and then stitch down that left side ¼" from the edge.

5. Tuck a few cards of thread in the pocket behind the pincushion, add a few colorful pins and a sampling of fresh needles, and slip in a new pair of little scissors. Because of the slight weight from the pincushion, this little needle book will stay open when you need it, and you can tie the ribbons to keep it closed when it is not in use.

Monogram Pinboard

As children grow and mature, so do their styles and tastes. A quick way to update their bedroom décor is with a fresh cover for a bulletin board personalized with their initials. Start by inviting them to select the fabrics, then have them help with simple straight-line sewing, and finally finish with a bit of handiwork to pull the whole thing together. These blocks make it easy to switch out the colors over time, and you can someday combine the collection of squares to create an heirloom monogram quilt sewn by both of you over the years.

FINISHED MEASUREMENTS

12" × 12" each

NOTES

- At its simplest, these paper-piecing blocks involve numbers and letters. You will piece fabric to the paper, working the numbered areas in order within each lettered section, and then join the lettered sections.

- If you are still unsure about paper-piecing quilt blocks, I suggest that you look online to find a video tutorial that works for you. (That is how I learned!)

- Shorten the stitch length on your machine to 1.5 because the increased perforations will simplify tearing away the paper.

- Seam allowances are ¼" unless otherwise noted.

- Backstitch at the beginning and end unless otherwise noted.

WHAT YOU NEED

12" × 12" cork tile

Monogram Pinboard paper-piecing letter templates (see the Templates section, pages 136–138)

An assortment of fabric scraps

Fabric in a complementary color for the sashing: (4 pieces) 6" × 14"

Rotary cutter and self-healing mat, or scissors

Flat-head thumbtacks

12" × 12" picture frame

HOW TO MAKE

1. Choose and copy a letter template and enlarge it to at least 8½" × 8½".

2. Select a piece of fabric that is slightly larger than Area 1 on your template. Place the fabric right side down on your work surface and then place the template right side up on top of it. Sew directly on top of the template, stitching the paper to the fabric and stitching along all the lines bordering Area 1. Press the fabric with an iron to set the stitches. Fold the paper back from the seam and trim the fabric ¼" from each line of stitches.

3. Now select a scrap of fabric about the size of Area 2 and place it right sides together with the fabric from Area 1, aligning the edges closest to the border between Areas 1 and 2. Turn the template right side up and stitch along the line between Areas 1 and 2. As before, press the fabric to set the stitches and then fold the paper back from the seam and trim the fabric ¼" from the line of stitches.

4. Continue stitching fabric pieces to additional areas on your paper template in this manner until the letter block is complete. Trim it to 8½" × 8½".

5. Add the sashing fabric strips to the paper-pieced block. Place 1 strip along the top of the block with right sides together, and sew along the edge. Repeat on the bottom of the block. Press the seams open on the reverse and then press again on the right side.

6. Add the sashing strips to both sides as you did for the top and bottom, and then press the finished block on both sides and trim it to about 14" × 14". Carefully tear away the paper from the reverse of the finished block and press both sides one more time.

7. Place the quilt block face down on your work surface and center a cork tile on top. (You are looking at the back of the pinboard.) Wrap the sashing edges over to the back of the cork tile and secure with flat-head thumbtacks.

8. To display, secure the tile in an empty frame and hang it on the wall with a few cute pushpins ready to go.

Legacy Quilt

A wonderful way to commemorate high school graduation or embarking on college/ university career is with a handmade lap quilt sporting bold, modern stripes in school colors. This cozy blanket can be used to keep loved ones warm while watching the big game, comfortable while enjoying a picnic on the quad with friends, or snug within the walls of a new home. Dare I say, this piece has a bit more style than traditional team blankets, and being handmade guarantees it will stand the test of time. Sure, the hand-stitching may take you a season to complete, but all the while you will be warm and comfortable under a blanket of school colors as you carefully and lovingly stitch a very special piece that will accompany a young adult to the next adventure.

FINISHED MEASUREMENTS
About 44" × 60"

NOTES

- Prewash all fabrics prior to cutting to allow for shrinkage.

- Seam allowances are ¼" unless otherwise noted.

- Backstitch at the beginning and end unless otherwise noted.

WHAT YOU NEED

44"-wide solid color quilting cotton: 1 yard each in four colors (4 yards total)

Quilting cotton in a coordinating color for the backing fabric: 2 yards

Cotton batting: (1 piece) 45" × 60" (crib size)

Thread in coordinating colors

Walking foot for your sewing machine (optional, but very helpful)

Embroidery needles

Embroidery floss in coordinating colors

HOW TO MAKE

1. Cut your fabrics from selvedge to selvedge and label them accordingly:

   - 2 pieces of fabric A measuring 5" × width of fabric (A1)
   - 1 piece of fabric A measuring 10" × width of fabric (A2)
   - 2 pieces of fabric B measuring 10" × width of fabric (B1)
   - 1 piece of fabric B measuring 2½" × width of fabric (B2)
   - 2 pieces of fabric C measuring 2½" × width of fabric (C1)
   - 1 piece of fabric C measuring 5" × width of fabric (C2)
   - 2 pieces of fabric D measuring 5" × width of fabric (D1)
   - 1 piece of fabric D measuring 10" × width of fabric (D2)

2. Lay out 1 piece of each type of fabric strip on a large work surface so that the colors and fabric widths are varied (A1, B1, C1, D1, A2, B2, C2, D2) or in any order that is pleasing to you. Work in pairs to piece the strips with their right sides together. Join the pairs and continue in this manner until all the fabric is pieced together. Press the seams to 1 side on the reverse and then press the seams again on the right side. When complete, you will have a piece measuring approximately 46½" × the width of the fabric.

3. Now piece the remaining 4 fabric strips (A1, B1, C1, D1) together just as you did before. Press the seams to 1 side on the reverse and then press again on the right side. When complete, you will have a piece measuring approximately 21" × the width of the fabric.

4. Place the the two pieced fabrics right sides together, making sure the stripes on each piece run perpenticular to each other. Sew the pieces together and press the new seam on both sides. Trim the piece to measure 42" × 62".

Assembly

5. Place the quilt top right side up on a flat surface. Then place the backing fabric right side down on top of the quilt top. Finally, place the batting on top of the quilt backing. Pin around the entire perimeter of the quilt. (*Note: A nice way to echo the colors of the quilt top on the reverse is to incorporate patchwork trimmings into the backing fabric of the quilt. I simply pieced the excess strips [from trimming the top] to the backing fabric and then cut it to size.*)

6. Stitch around the perimeter of the quilt sandwich using a ½" seam allowance, leaving an 8" opening on one side for turning.

7. Reach inside the opening between the quilt top and backing fabric and flip the entire piece right side out so that the batting is sandwiched between the quilt top and the backing fabric. Gently push out the corners of the quilt using your finger or a chopstick. Press the entire piece with a steam iron. Pin the opening closed.

8. (*Note: I highly recommend using a walking foot on your sewing machine from this point on. It will help to keep the top and bottom fabrics properly aligned while machine-stitching.*) Topstitch the entire piece ¼" in from the edge. Work slowly when you reach the section with the pinned opening to ensure you securely closed it.

Quilting

9. Baste the quilt using pins or long basting stitches with a needle and thread.

10. Machine quilt parallel to the stripes at 3" to 6" intervals using coordinating colored threads.

11. Use embroidery floss in contrasting colors to hand quilt running stitches ½" to the side of each seam.

Finishing

12. Wash the quilt in warm water and tumble dry on medium heat to shrink the batting and give the quilt that well-loved, crinkly look.

Strawberry Lemonade Schorle

It is a tradition for my daughters and me to pick strawberries every June. We enjoy supporting our local farms, getting out in the fields, and, of course, sampling berries right off the vine. One time we came home with close to thirty pounds of berries, but most years we show a bit more restraint. Upon arriving home, we clean and freeze at least half of our haul to be enjoyed in the middle of winter when we need a reminder of warmer days. Then we enjoy strawberry everything: muffins, parfaits, and, of course, freezer jam. Our favorite way to savor the flavor on hot summer days, however, is to make Schorle that tastes like summer. Schorle is a German drink made by diluting juice (or wine) with sparkling mineral water, much like what we in America refer to as a spritzer. The most popular variation is Apfelschorle, which is a combination of apple juice and sparkling mineral water.

A batch of this strawberry lemonade purée has the potential to last in the fridge about a week, but we have never been able to make it last longer than a day or two. This Schorle is a bit sweet, a bit sour, cool, and bubbly . . . the perfect refreshment!

Strawberry Lemonade Schorle

INGREDIENTS

- 2 pints strawberries, washed and hulled
- 6 to 8 lemons
- 1 cup sugar
- Seltzer, sparkling mineral water, or club soda
- Spirits, such as vodka, bourbon, tequila, gin, or rum (optional)

PREPARATION

To make the purée base, squeeze the juice from the lemons until you have 1 cup of lemon juice, and pour it into a bowl. Add the sugar and allow it to dissolve (stirring as needed).

Crush the strawberries in a separate bowl using a potato masher until they reach the consistency of purée that you like (we like ours with a bit of texture, but you could use a food processor to make a smoother purée). Combine the sugar/lemon mixture with the strawberries, pour it into a lidded jar, and refrigerate.

FOR THE KIDS

Spoon ¼ cup of the purée into the bottom of a glass. Pour 6 ounces of seltzer over the purée and stir to combine. Add ice cubes and serve with a straw and a long spoon so you can enjoy every bit of the berryliciousness.

FOR THE GROWN-UPS

Fill a cocktail shaker with ice. Spoon in ¼ cup of the purée and 2 ounces of your favorite spirits, and shake well. Pour (strained or not) into your favorite cocktail glass and top with 2 ounces of seltzer.

TO HONOR

the Past

A few generations ago, it was common to own a family trunk that quite literally was handed down from generation to generation. During a recent trip to New York City, the historical value of trunks like these hit home for me. While visiting Ellis Island—the busiest gateway for immigrants coming to the United States from the late 1800s to the mid-1900s—we viewed the archives documenting immigrants arriving after long and exhausting voyages. The exhibits depicted seemingly endless lines of people with storage trunks in tow, much like the barrel top trunk that is in my own parents' home today. In search of a brighter future, many of our ancestors ventured across the ocean—traveling only with what would fit in their trunk—and left everything else behind.

Take a moment to consider: If you had to do the same, what would you pack in your trunk? How do you honor your past? And how do you hope others will remember you? A century from now, all the gadgets we use so frequently today will simply be artifacts of what once was. Instead of creating a time capsule, I propose choosing to fill your metaphorical trunk with memories, like the first "real" sweaters you ever knit. Treasure the items with rich histories unique to you and your family. Open your trunk often and let each piece share its story. Create a home filled with heirloom-quality comforts where you can put your feet up, surrounded by gifts from the heart, and exhale after a long day. Create that legacy for your family and friends . . . and for posterity.

Memory Tiles

I have fond memories of flipping through family photos while growing up. It was a fun way to reminisce about good times spent with friends and family who lived far away. The transition to digital cameras, while incredibly accessible and convenient, has regretfully made many of us a bit lazy when it comes to organizing our photos. I am as guilty of this as the next person and do not print nearly enough photos, and our photo albums are sorely lacking in organization. (But that is a priority of mine for the coming year, I swear!) This project is intended as a gentle reminder of just how simple it is to display photos of our loved ones in creative ways: a personalized version of the quintessential Concentration game featuring the faces of friends and family. The game is fun for all ages and is also good exercise for our memories as we get older (ahem). Come to think of it, perhaps if I play enough, I may even remember to work on our photo albums.

FINISHED MEASUREMENTS
2" × 2" each

NOTES

- If you prefer not to cut the balsa wood tiles yourself, you can use premade 2" tiles and skip ahead to Step 3.

- A set of memory tiles makes a great gift. Place them in a vintage tin box along with some blank tiles, a paintbrush and small jar of decoupage medium, and handwritten directions so the recipients can add to his or her collection of memory tiles over the years.

HOW TO MAKE

1. Measure and cut the balsa wood into 2" squares using a craft knife on a self-healing mat.

2. Smooth the edges of each balsa wood piece using a sanding block. When finished, wipe each tile with a slightly damp cloth to remove any dust. Allow the wood to dry.

3. Scan and print 2 copies of each photo, keeping in mind that the main image should be no larger than 2" × 2". Cut the images to size.

4. Use a paintbrush to apply a thin layer of decoupage medium to the top of 1 square and place the image on top. Smooth out any air bubbles with your fingers and then apply a coat of the decoupage medium over the entire image. Allow the image to dry completely.

5. Apply a top coat to seal each tile, and allow the tiles to dry before playing the game.

WHAT YOU NEED

Balsa wood: (1 piece)
³/₁₆" × 4" × 36" (see Note)

Ruler

Craft knife and a self-healing mat

Fine-grit soft sanding block

An assortment of photos

Scanner and color copier, or consider printing the images at your local copy shop. (Samples shown were printed on matte photo paper with a basic home inkjet printer. The photos were clear and the ink did not smudge even the slightest bit when decoupaged.)

Paintbrushes

Decoupage medium (such as Mod Podge)

Cameo Brooch

Cameos have been admired as art and worn as jewelry for more than two thousand years. The traditional method involved carving stone, bone, gemstone, or shell to reveal layers of contrasting colors while creating the desired image. You may even have an heirloom cameo that has been handed down through your own family. Pieces like these are valuable connections with our past. This project is a simplified and modern version made using, of all things, shrink plastic. These silhouette pins have both artistic and sentimental value, as they portray images of beloved family members, friends, and even pets in one-of-a-kind jewelry to be worn and shared.

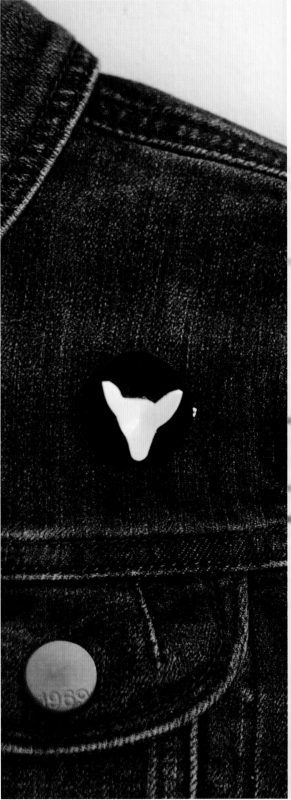

FINISHED MEASUREMENTS
Sizes vary

NOTE

- If you can find a brooch pin-back with a bail for pendant attachment, the cameo can be worn as either a pin or necklace.

HOW TO MAKE

1. Trace a 3½" to 4" circle on clear shrink plastic. Use a black permanent marker to color in the sanded (rough) side. Set aside.

2. Place the sheet of white shrink plastic on top of the profile photo and trace the outline of the silhouette.

3. Use a craft knife and a self-healing mat (or fine scissors) to carefully cut out the silhouette for the cameo.

4. Place both pieces on a foil-lined baking sheet with a few inches of space between them. Follow the manufacturer's instructions to shrink the plastic in the oven. Allow the plastic to cool completely.

5. Center the white silhouette on the black circle and affix it with a strong, permanent craft glue. Allow the glue to dry.

6. Use the same craft glue to attach a brooch pin-back to the back of the cameo. Allow the glue to dry completely before wearing the cameo.

WHAT YOU NEED

Shrink plastic sheets (such as Shrinky Dinks or PolyShrink): 1 sheet each of white and clear

Black permanent marker

3" profile (head or silhouette) photo of who is to be portrayed in the cameo

Craft knife and a self-healing mat (or fine scissors)

Cookie sheet covered with aluminum foil

Permanent craft glue (such as E-6000)

Brooch pin-back (see Note)

Carrie's Ring Dish

One of my oldest and dearest friends gave me a lovely little ring dish on my wedding day. More than fifteen years later, it still sits on my dresser where each night I place my rings for safekeeping. It was such a simple and thoughtful gift, and each day it reminds me of my childhood friend and all the memories we share. A sweet, personalized gift like this is simple to craft by hand for someone special in your life, and the gesture will be cherished for a lifetime.

FINISHED MEASUREMENTS
4" diameter

NOTES

- Not all oven-bake clays are the same. Some are softer and easier to work with than others, and I suggest trying out a few to find the one you will prefer.

- Follow the manufacturer's baking instructions on your particular clay to be certain the finished piece will be properly cured.

HOW TO MAKE

1. Preheat the oven to the manufacturer's recommended temperature for the clay.

2. Place a piece of wax or parchment paper on your work surface to protect it.

3. Knead the clay in your hands and form it into a ball. Use the rolling pin to roll out the clay to a thickness of about ¼". To ensure the clay will have an even thickness, place 2 pencils on the table on either side of the clay and ease the rolling pin down over top of them.

4. Use letter stamps to create impressions in the clay, such as initials or a special message.

5. Place the cookie cutter on the clay and press down firmly to cut the circle for the bowl. (If you are using a circular lid, place the lid on top of the clay and trace around it with a craft knife to cut out the circle.) Remove the excess clay from around the sides and then carefully remove the cookie cutter. Lightly smooth the round edge with your fingertips.

6. Place the clay in the oven-safe bowl and gently press the clay into the bottom of the bowl.

7. Place the bowl on a cookie sheet and put it in the oven. Bake the clay according to the manufacturer's instructions. Remove the cookie sheet from the oven and allow your dish to remain inside the oven-safe bowl until it cools completely (overnight is best). When the bowl has cooled, turn it over and your dish should come right out.

8. Use the sanding block to smooth the edges of the bowl, if desired.

WHAT YOU NEED

Oven-bake clay (such as Sculpey or Fimo): 2-oz package

Wax or parchment paper

Alphabet stamps

Rolling pin

Two standard-size pencils, chopsticks, or short ¼" dowels about 8" in length

4" round cookie cutter (or circular lid and a craft knife)

Oven-safe bowl

Cookie sheet

Fine-grit soft buffing block (like the kind used for a manicure)

Keepsake Bins

For as long as we have been married, my husband has left me a little note before he goes to work. Those few words scribbled on a piece of scratch paper bring a smile to my face each morning. It is nothing fancy, and each new note almost always says the same thing; yet they each mean so much to me. I have saved them all over the years, and keep them in a simple bin on my dresser. I love the ritual of it all: he writes the note before sunrise (and leaves it by the coffeemaker, thank you!); I find it a few hours later and place it with the others on my dresser, adding to my collection of reminders that I am loved.

These bins are a wonderful way to corral your keepsakes, organize your needlework, gather your collections, or simply tidy up around the house. The knit bins are a nice complement to their sewn counterparts, and a combination of both would look especially great when made with coordinating colors. A set makes a lovely heirloom gift and is a nice way for nearly everyone to highlight his or her own treasures and keepsakes.

Knit Bins

FINISHED MEASUREMENTS

8" wide × 6" deep × 4" high (when folded)

NOTES

- Knit with two strands of yarn at all times. I use a yarn swift + ball winder to wind skeins into center-pull "cakes" and then knit with the inside and outside strands simultaneously. If you do not have these tools, your local yarn shop will most likely wind it for you free of charge when purchasing yarn.

- You really do not need to be concerned with gauge for this project. Seriously! The knitted basket will be larger than expected and quite floppy when the knitting is complete, but the fibers will shrink and intertwine during the felting process to form a dense, firm fabric.

HOW TO MAKE

CO 18 sts in the MC.
Sl 1, k17. Repeat for a total of 54 rows to create a garter stitch rectangle.
Use your working needle to pick up 25 sts down one long side of the piece and then pick up 18 sts on the other short end and 25 sts on the other long side (86 sts total).

PM and join to work in the round, being careful not to twist sts.
Knit for 18 rounds, or until you run out of the MC yarn.
Switch to CC yarn and knit for 6 rounds.
Purl for 3 rounds.
BO all sts.

Felt the bin (see Knitting and Crochet Abbreviations + Tutorials, page 145). While the bin is still damp after felting, fold over the top edge by 1". Use your hands to stretch, tug, and form the felted wool into a box shape. Place a folded towel inside the bin and allow it to dry completely. Trim any stray strands of yarn.

WHAT YOU NEED

Yarn

220 yards of worsted weight 100% wool yarn in main color (MC)

About 100 yards of worsted weight 100% wool yarn in a contrasting color (CC)

Sample shown was knit using 1 skein of *Cascade 220 [100% Peruvian Highland wool; 220 yds (201 m) / 100 g]* in color 8509 Gray and <1 skein in color 820 Lemon.

Needles + Notions

US #11 / 8 mm 24" circular needle

Stitch markers

Sewn Bins

FINISHED MEASUREMENTS

About 10" wide × 6" deep × 10" high

NOTES

- I prefer not to use interfacing in my sewn bins. As you can imagine, they are pretty floppy when empty; however, once filled they hold their shape just fine and have just the right amount of slouch that I like. That said, if you prefer a bin with a more structured shape, adhere a layer of fusible interfacing to the back of the main fabric before cutting.

- Prewash fabrics to allow for shrinkage prior to cutting.

- Seam allowances are ¼" unless otherwise noted.

- Backstitch at the beginning and end unless otherwise noted.

- These bins are fully reversible! No matter which side faces out, the interior fabric will also be showcased in the fold-over cuff, so be sure to pick a lining fabric that you like.

WHAT YOU NEED

Cotton or linen fabric: ½ yard

Cotton fabric in a complementary color/print for the lining: ½ yard (see Note)

Lightweight fusible interfacing: ½ yard (optional; see Note)

HOW TO MAKE

1. Cut two 15" × 15" pieces each of the main and lining fabrics.

2. Place the 2 main fabric pieces right sides together and pin along the bottom and both sides. Sew the pieces together, leaving the top open. Press both sides.

3. Trace and cut out a 2½" square in each of the bottom corners using the stitch lines as a guide for measuring. Open up one corner and bring together the cut edges on the bottom and side seams, right sides together, to flatten the corner. Pin the side and bottom seams to opposite sides to reduce bulk and press. Repeat this step with the other corner, and then stitch both bottom corners using a ½" seam allowance to create the gusset. Press all sides.

4. Repeat Steps 2 and 3 with the lining fabric pieces, but leave a 3" opening for turning along the bottom edge of the lining in Step 2.

5. Place the lining piece right side out and inside the main fabric piece so that their right sides are together. Pin the pieces together around the entire top edge, taking care to align the seams. Sew the top edge using a ½" seam allowance. Press to set the stitches.

6. Reach inside through the opening in the lining to turn the bin right side out. Push your hand into the corners of the gussets to shape them.

7. Pin and sew closed the opening in the lining using a ¼" seam allowance or sew by hand using a blind stitch.

8. Place the lining inside, and press the top edge with an iron. Topstitch all the way around the top ¼" from the edge to secure the fabrics to one another with a neat, finished look. Press the bin inside and out to set the stitches.

9. Fold down the top edge of the bin by 2½" to 3" to expose the lining fabric.

Knitting Needle Roll

Over time, I have been lucky enough to inherit several sets of double pointed knitting needles. One set of the thinnest metal needles came from my mother, along with tales of knitting argyle socks while waiting in the cafeteria line at Penn State. While I have not yet been ambitious enough to knit something so intricate (although never say never), I have become quite a fan of using double pointed needles in my own handwork. Until recently I stored all of my knitting needles, new and old, in one mismatched bunch in an antique canister atop the armoire that houses my yarn stash. Then one day, I decided to whip up a simple needle roll to neatly store all those lovely double pointed needles. Not only does it make me happy to see them all and remember those who shared them with me, but organizing them this way allows me to easily see what sizes of needles I have on hand. Someday, when my needles are handed down, they will be inside this very needle roll.

FINISHED MEASUREMENTS
About 17" × 17" when opened, and 9" long when rolled

NOTES

- Prewash fabrics to allow for shrinkage prior to cutting.

- Seam allowances are ¼" unless otherwise noted.

- Backstitch at the beginning and end unless otherwise noted.

- For the sleeve, 1" wide gingham fabric is extremely cute and it also provides guidelines for stitching the individual slots in the sleeve.

WHAT YOU NEED

Fabric for the exterior:
1 fat quarter yard

Fabric for the lining:
1 fat quarter yard

Fabric for the sleeve:
1 fat quarter yard (see Note)

Scrap fabric or ribbon:
(2 pieces) about ¾" × 15"

Water-soluble marking pen

HOW TO MAKE

1. Cut 1 piece each of the exterior and lining fabrics measuring 18" × 18" and then cut 1 piece of the sleeve fabric measuring 18" × 14".

2. Fold the sleeve fabric in half, wrong sides together, along the length of the fabric (so it measures 18" × 7" when folded) and press along the crease. Topstitch along the fold ⅛" from the edge. Press both sides.

3. With the lining fabric right side up on your work surface, place the folded sleeve piece on top of it with the bottom raw edges aligned. Place the 2 fabric strips on top of the sleeve fabric about 5" up from the bottom so that their length extends across the sleeve area. Pin all around to secure the fabrics together and then topstitch along the bottom and 2 short sides ⅛" from the edge. Press both sides.

4. Place the lining piece and exterior fabric piece with right sides together and pin along all 4 sides. Use a ½" seam allowance to sew all around the perimeter of the piece, leaving a 4" opening on one side for turning. Iron both sides to set the stitches. Clip the corners and turn the piece right side out, carefully pulling out the ties and pushing out the corners. Press both sides again.

5. Pin the opening shut and then topstitch ⅛" from the edge all around the piece.

6. With the lining and sleeve side facing up, use a ruler and water-soluble pen to mark lines to divide the individual sections anywhere from 1" to 2" wide. Topstitch along these lines and press the entire piece on both sides one last time.

7. Slide double pointed needles into their sections according to size, fold the top fabric over the sleeve, roll it up, and secure it with the ties.

Generation Swatch Blanket

Those of us who knit and crochet amass a collection of swatches over the years. These unassuming squares are tremendously helpful in determining gauge, pattern, and color placement when embarking on new projects. But they are also handcrafted snapshots of our personal histories as makers. Though small in size, each swatch is a reminder of something made for others; and when combined, they tell a story. This swatch blanket can begin small with reminders of sweet baby knits and will ultimately grow in size over time to include swatches from hand-knit treasures made during school years and beyond. Consider this blanket an ongoing project that you may, in fact, never truly complete . . . and that is the best part of it. The addition of each new swatch block contributes to a warm embrace that transcends time.

Although each swatch will be completely different, the main yarn bordering each will anchor the piece with color and texture. Incorporating a neutral tone as the main color showcases each of the swatches. The "finished" piece can be enjoyed as a small, lovely blanket for an infant and combined with others to grow in size and someday cover an entire bed. Instead of an "I spy" quilt, this blanket is a trip down memory lane, filled with hand-knit snapshots of each piece made over time.

FINISHED MEASUREMENTS

Sizes vary

STITCH PATTERN

Seed Stitch (work with an even number or sts)

Row 1 (RS): K1, p1 to the end of row.

Row 2 (WS): P1, k1 to the end of the row.

WHAT YOU NEED

Yarn

Worsted weight wool (amounts vary) (Sample shown features swatches knit using various yarns showcased among natural off-white stripes of *Patons Classic Wool [100% pure new wool; 210 yds (192 m) / 100 g]* in color Aran.)

Needles + Notions

US #7 / 4.5 mm needles

Tapestry needle

Gauge

6 sts = 1" (2.5 cm) in Seed Stitch (see Stitch Pattern)

NOTES

- This project features a method more than a pattern, per se. As such, there will be variations in the gauge of the smaller swatches versus the gauge of the joining panels. The instructions below call upon simple math skills to calculate the appropriate number of stitches to pick up for joining each new swatch to the larger piece.

- Worsted weight wool is my preferred yarn for filling out each row, as it marries well with both finer- and thicker-gauged swatches.

HOW TO MAKE

1. Begin by taking the measurements of 1 swatch to determine its size. Determine the amount of sts to pick up as follows: length of side of swatch in inches × sts per inch in the new yarn's gauge. For example, if the side you are working on is 4" long and your gauge is 6 sts per inch, then you will pick up 24 sts evenly along this side.

2. Pick up and knit sts evenly on one side: Working with 1 needle, with RS facing and starting with the edge of the st on the top right corner, insert the needle from front to back through the st. Wrap the yarn around the needle as if to knit and pull the st back through the loop. Now insert the needle through the next st (to the left of the st just picked up), and pick up and knit another st in the same manner. Repeat this step to pick up and knit the number of sts you calculated are needed for that specific edge.

3. Work Seed Stitch (see Stitch Pattern, page 109) on this one side until the entire piece measures anywhere between 4" to 10" in length. BO all sts.

4. Now pick up the same number of sts along the opposite side of the swatch and work Seed Stitch back and forth until the piece measures 24" in length. BO all sts and then block the piece.

5. Repeat with additional swatches, adjusting the number of sts picked up according to the measurement of each swatch and always working to 24" total length. Vary the length of each side of new knitting so that when the pieces are joined the swatches will be placed randomly rather

than at set intervals. Once you have at least 4 swatch bands completed, block them and weave in the ends.

6. Use a tapestry needle and yarn to join the panels at their long sides, varying the position of the swatches in each adjacent row: Place the edges side by side with RS facing down. Stitch up the sides in alternating rows by pulling the needle through the purl loops at the ends of the rows. When seamed, weave in any loose ends and block to smooth out any irregularities.

7. Create additional bands over time as new swatches become available and add them to the blanket as before. Eventually, you can join four 24" × 24" blankets to create a 48" × 48" lap blanket. Add another pair of swatch blankets later to create a blanket for a twin bed.

Time Capsule Pillow

A few bits of fabric or yarn invariably remain when any given project is complete. These leftovers accumulate over time, are connected to projects that are out there in the world—sweaters made for new babies, hats and mittens made for loved ones, and so on—and it would be a shame to see them go to waste. Long after those lovingly stitched pieces are outgrown and packed away with other heirlooms to be handed down, this pillow will remain in your home like a scrapbook of snapshots, each color of yarn or strip of fabric a memory of handcrafted pieces made for special people. Whether you make a crocheted bolster, sew a square pillow, or decide to do both, this piece will remind the recipient of lovely moments from the past and is certain to be enjoyed each and every day for years to come.

Sewn Pillow

FINISHED MEASUREMENTS
Sized to fit a 16" square pillow

NOTES

- This project uses a variation of the "quilt as you go" method I learned about in Suzuko Koseki's book *Patchwork Style,* and later used in my book *Vintage Made Modern.* Fabric strips are stitched directly to a piece of batting, building up layers to outline the center square. When finished, you trim the block to size.

- Prewash all fabrics prior to cutting to allow for shrinkage.

- Seam allowances are ¼" unless otherwise noted.

- Backstitch at the beginning and end unless otherwise noted.

HOW TO MAKE

1. Place the quilt batting on your work surface. Position the center square of fabric right side up directly in the middle of the batting and pin it in place. Stitch the fabric square to the batting on all 4 sides ¼" in from the edges. Press it in place.

2. Cut a 3" length of Fabric A. Place this strip on top of the center square with right sides together, align their 3" sides, and pin them in place. Sew the fabrics together and then press the seam open.

3. Continue adding strips of Fabric A in this manner—adding pieces to each side, then the top and bottom—increasing the length of each strip as needed. Each time you sew a new strip to the block with right sides together, press the seam open. Once the center square is bordered on all 4 sides with strips of Fabric A, begin sewing strips of Fabric B in the same manner, then Fabric C, and finally Fabric D.

4. Press well on both sides and then quilt by machine or hand in a pattern that is pleasing to you. I like to do a sequence of straight-line stitching using threads in coordinating colors. When you are finished, trim the quilted block to 17" × 17".

5. Place 1 backing fabric piece on the quilted block with right sides together and the edges aligned. Sew the pieces together along one 17" edge and press the seam open. Repeat this step on the other side with the other piece of backing fabric. The main piece should now be 17" × 40".

6. Now place the lining and the main piece right sides together. Pin and sew around all sides leaving a 5" opening for turning along 1 long side. Clip the corners and turn the piece right side out, pushing gently into the corners with the end of a paintbrush or a chopstick. Press well on both sides.

7. Topstitch both short ends ¼" in from the edges to give it a clean finished look.

8. With the main fabric facing up, fold the 2 short sides toward the center so that they overlap by about 7". Pin along the top and bottom edges. Sew along the top and bottom edges. Turn the pillow cover right side out.

9. Wash and dry the pillow cover for a cozy, crinkly, quilted look, if desired.

10. Insert the pillow form through the opening and give it a little squeeze to even out the stuffing.

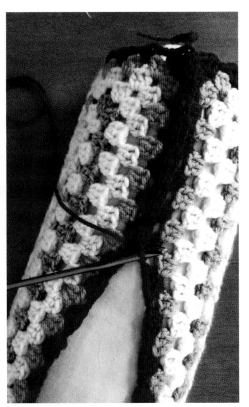

Crocheted Pillow

FINISHED MEASUREMENTS

Sized to fit a 16" bolster pillow

HOW TO MAKE

Start with color A.

Make a slip knot.

CH 5 and then connect to form a loop using a slip stitch in the first stitch of the chain.

CH 3 (this will serve as the first DC in the round).

DC 11 through the center of the loop, and then connect with the first CH3 using a slip stitch in the first stitch of the chain. Cut the yarn with a tail of about 5".

There should be 12 DC in color A.

Switch to color B.

CH 3 between any 2 of the DC (this will serve as the first DC in the round), then DC 2 more times in that same space. CH 3 (this will be the corner), then DC 3 times (again) through that same space. CH 3.

*Count over 3 DC in the previous loop (in color A) and DC 3 times into that space, CH 3 (corner in color B), then DC 3 more times through that same space, then CH 3. Repeat from * twice more, and then connect with the first DC using a slip stitch.

Cut the yarn with a tail of about 5".

There should be 24 DC in color B.

Switch to color C.

Start at one of the corner spaces (created with the CH 3 in color B).

WHAT YOU NEED

Yarn

Leftover bits of worsted weight yarns (The sample shown was made using oddballs of leftover yarns from sweaters and accessories I have knit and crocheted for my daughters over the years. See the Resources section, page 149, for a few of my favorite worsted weight yarns.)

Hooks + Notions

J-10 (6.0 mm) crochet hook

16" bolster pillow

Tapestry needle

CH 3 (this will serve as the first DC in the round), then DC 2 more times through that same space, then CH 3.

*DC 3 times into the next space (created by the CH 3 in color B), CH 3, then DC 3 times into the next corner space, CH 3 (corner for color C), and DC 3 more times into that same corner space. CH 3. Repeat from * twice more, and then DC 3 times into the next space, CH 3, DC 3 times into the final corner space, and CH 3. Connect with the first DC using a slip stitch.

Cut the yarn with a tail of about 5".

There should be 36 DC in color C.

Switch to color D.

Start at one of the corner spaces of color C.

CH 3 (this will serve as the first DC in the round), DC 2 more times through that same space, then CH 3.

*(DC 3 times into the next space, CH 3) 2 times, then DC 3 times into the next corner space, CH 3 (corner for color D), and DC 3 more times into that same corner space. CH 3. Repeat from * twice more, and then (DC 3 times into the next space, CH 3) 2 times, then DC 3 times into the final corner space, and CH 3. Connect with the first DC using a slip stitch.

Cut the yarn with a tail of about 5".

There should be 48 DC in color D.

Continue working in pattern, changing to a new color of yarn with each layer you add to the square, until the piece measures about 16" × 16".

Weave in and all of the ends and block to square.

Finishing   With the crocheted square face down on your work surface, center the bolster pillow on top. Thread a tapestry needle with yarn or use a crochet hook to stitch the crocheted square together so that it wraps around the length of the bolster. Then stitch the ends closed and use the yarn to gather and tie off both ends.

Doily Dream Catcher

Our Nana lived in our father's family home for most of my childhood. As best I can remember, it was an old house near the top of a hill with a big front porch and creaky wooden floors. We visited often, staying over for the weekend, spending time with her, and exploring the neighborhood streets of the small city where both of our parents had grown up. At night, I remember being a bit frightened by the sounds of the old house, and Nana always knew how to soothe my anxieties with imaginative stories and the very best tuck-in lullaby. It is a fond memory that I share with our daughters each evening by tucking them in just so.

Simple rituals like these can help assuage fears most of the time; however, there are nights when little ones among us can find it difficult to fall asleep. Whether it is related to separation anxiety, booming thunderstorms, or a bad dream, nighttime can be tough for kids. Making dream catchers is a creative solution and a simple project you can do together with your little night owl, and crafting together is a delightful process for all ages. A simple tuck-in and lullaby under a dream catcher might even lead to a good night's sleep for everyone involved.

FINISHED MEASUREMENTS
Sizes vary

NOTE

- Consider using an heirloom doily to enhance a personal connection with the dream catcher.

HOW TO MAKE

1. If using spray starch, apply it to the doily according to manufacturer's instructions.

2. Center the doily on top of the inner hoop and secure it by tightening the outer hoop around it. Adjust the position of the doily as needed.

3. Thread an assortment of embellishments onto lengths of twine and tie them along the bottom third of the curved edge of the hoop. You can also tie a few single beads to the center area of the doily.

4. When finished, talk about how the dream catcher will keep the bad dreams out and only the good, sweet dreams will pass through. Sweet dreams to all, and to all a good night!

WHAT YOU NEED

Cotton or linen doily (see Note)

Spray starch (optional)

Round wooden embroidery hoop slightly smaller than the doily

Linen or hemp twine

Embroidery needle (optional)

Various embellishments such as beads, trinkets, feathers, and the like

Apple Crisp

A fond memory from my childhood is the anticipation that would build up as we drove to the lake where my maternal grandparents lived. My grandfather was most often outside tinkering on his latest project while my grandmother was in the kitchen baking something special. It was her way of welcoming us into their home after a long drive. Even in her nineties, Grammy would bake apple pie or dumplings (and always brownies for my brother) to enjoy upon our arrival. As I think many people would agree, not much compares to the sweet aroma of freshly baked apple pie. And the scent of baking apples is especially sweet when it is connected to such special memories.

Apple Crisp

INGREDIENTS

- 6 apples
- Juice of 1 lemon
- 1 tablespoon cinnamon
- 2 tablespoons flour
- 2 tablespoons granulated sugar

FOR THE TOPPING

- ¾ cup flour
- ½ cup (1 stick) unsalted butter, cubed and kept cold
- 1 cup rolled oats
- ¾ cup brown sugar
- 1 teaspoon cinnamon
- ¼ teaspoon fresh nutmeg
- Pinch of salt
- Vanilla bean ice cream, to serve (optional)

PREPARATION

Preheat the oven to 350°. Butter an 8" × 8" casserole or pie plate.

Wash, core, and slice the apples and toss them with lemon juice. Mix the cinnamon with the flour and sugar. Sprinkle the mixture over the apples and toss the slices with your hands to cover. Pour the apples into the casserole.

To make the topping, add the flour to a mixing bowl and cut the butter into the flour with a fork or pastry blender until it resembles coarse sand. Add the oats, brown sugar, cinnamon, nutmeg, and salt and stir to combine. Crumble the topping over the apples.

Bake for 30 to 40 minutes or until topping is browned and crisp with the apples bubbling underneath.

Serve warm with a scoop of vanilla bean ice cream.

Templates

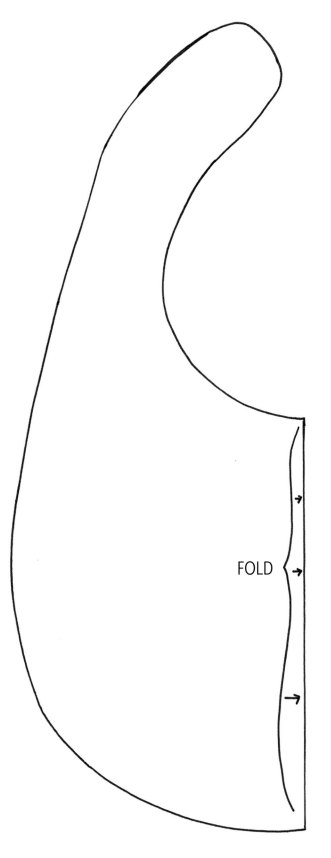

FOLD

123

WE
LCO
ME

Baby's Bunting

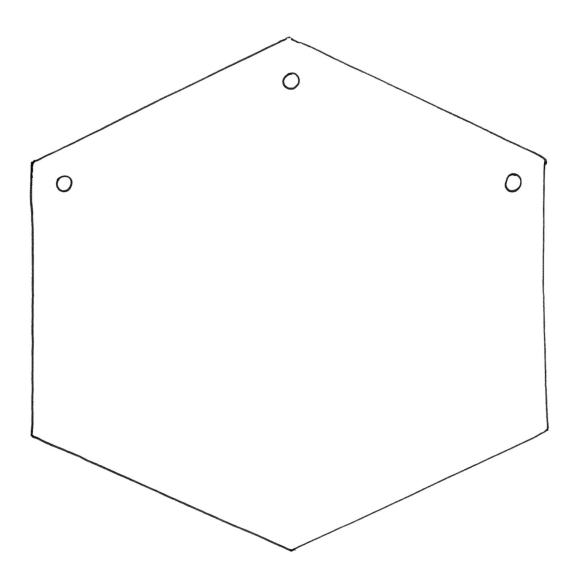

Flying Ace Aircraft

ENLARGE 130%

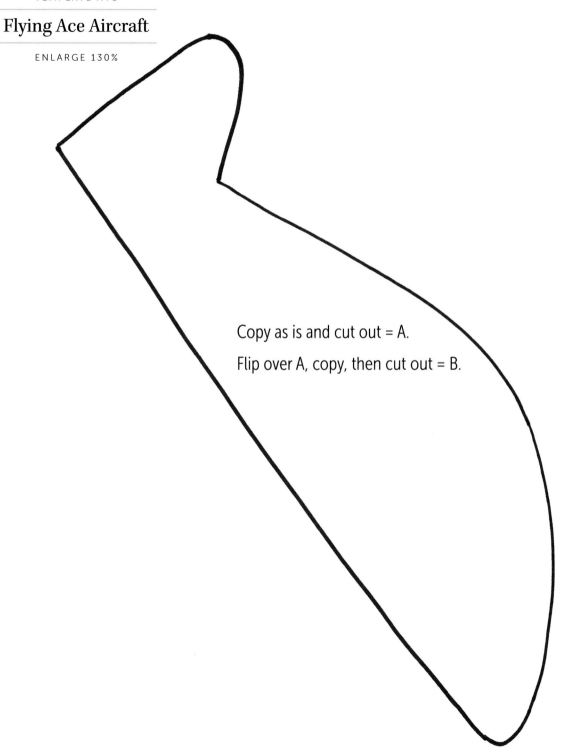

Copy as is and cut out = A.

Flip over A, copy, then cut out = B.

Flying Ace Aircraft

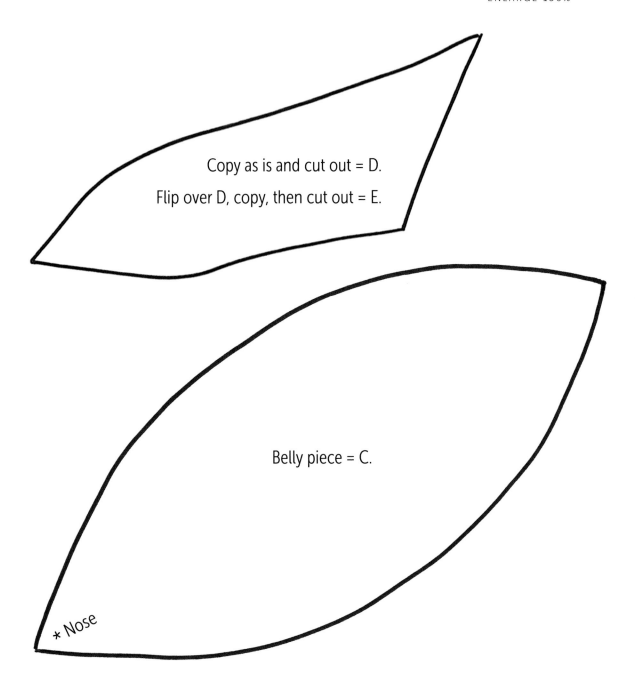

Copy as is and cut out = D.

Flip over D, copy, then cut out = E.

Belly piece = C.

* Nose

Soft Toy Anymal—Kitty

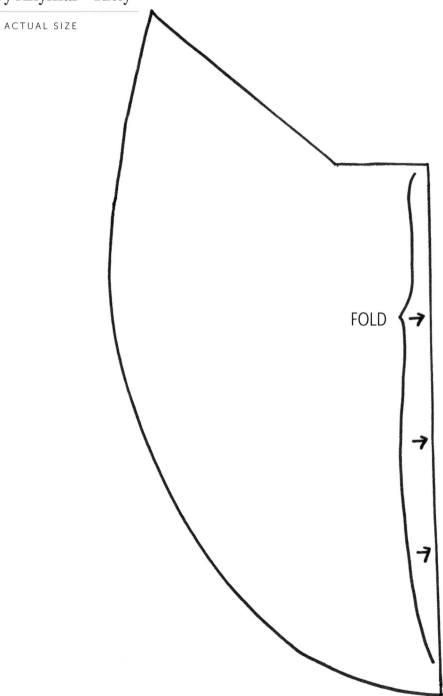

FOLD

Soft Toy Anymal—Mouse

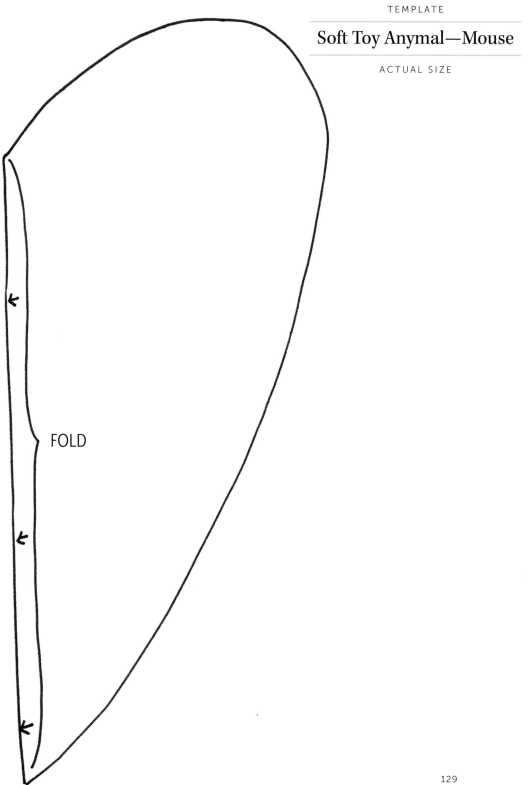

FOLD

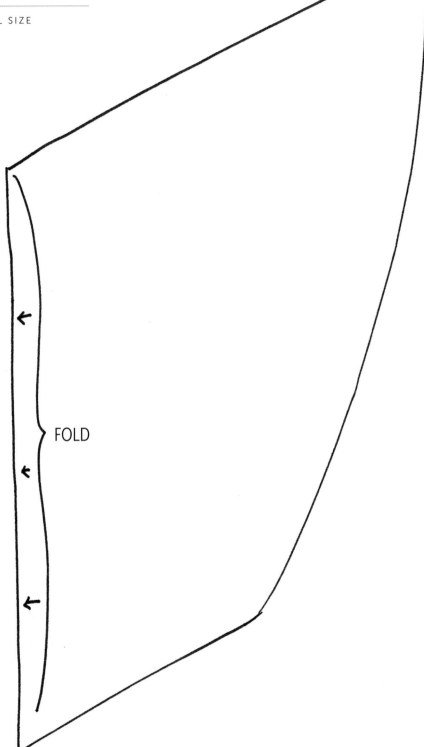

FOLD

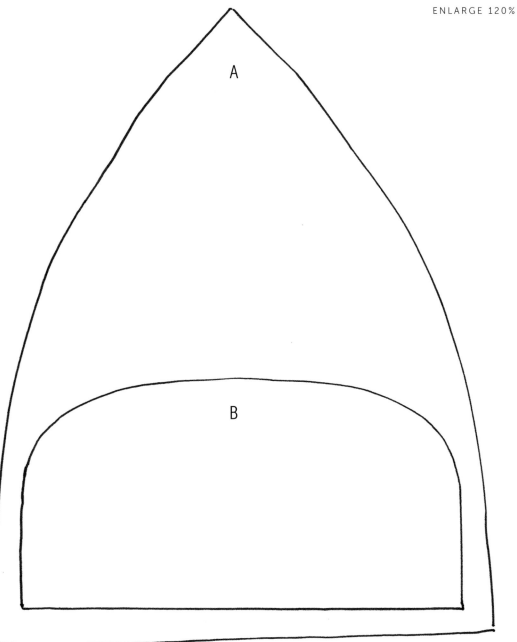

A

B

Popover Tunic

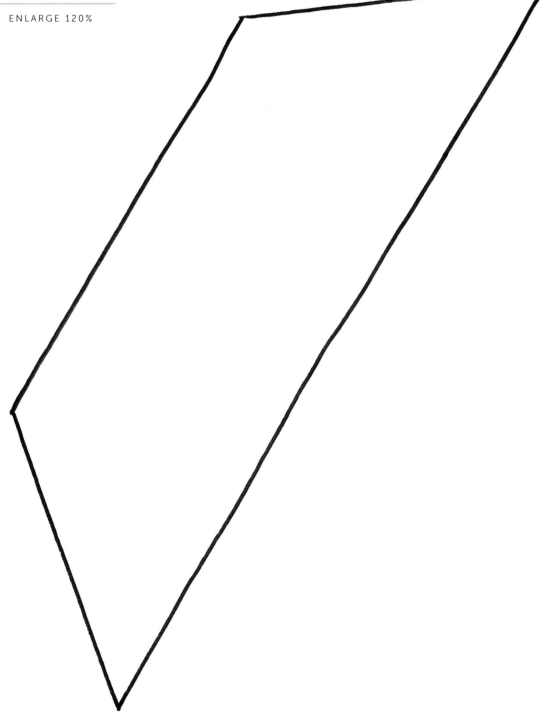

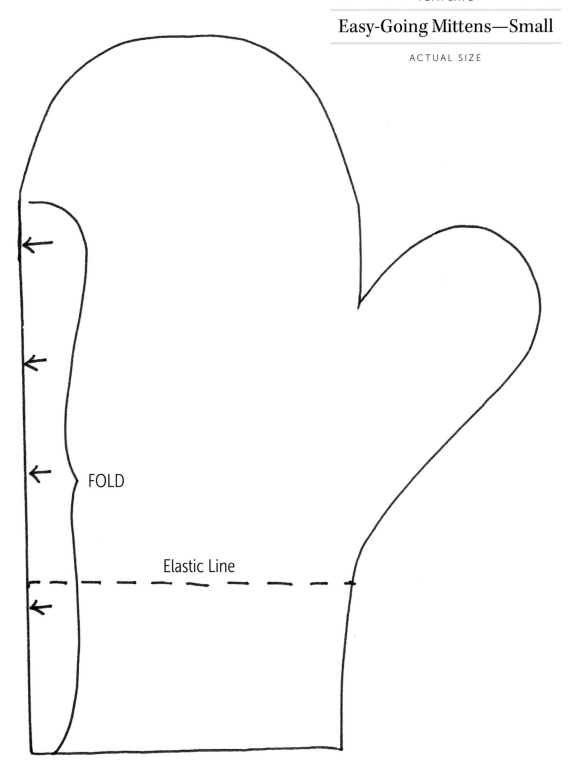

FOLD

Elastic Line

Easy-Going Mittens—Medium

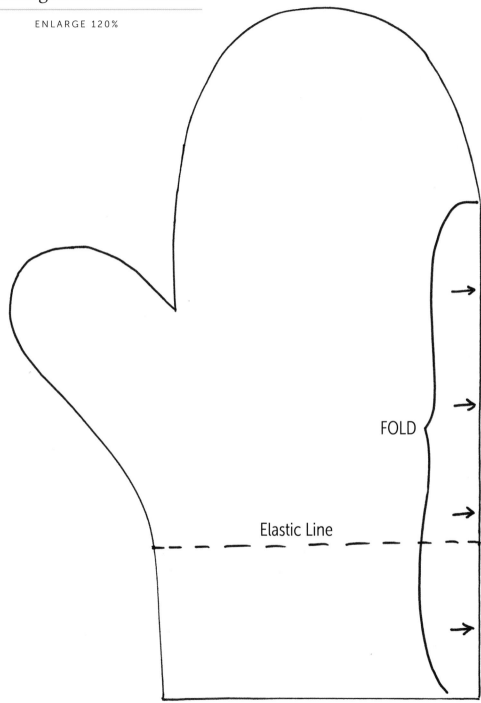

FOLD

Elastic Line

Easy-Going Mittens—Large

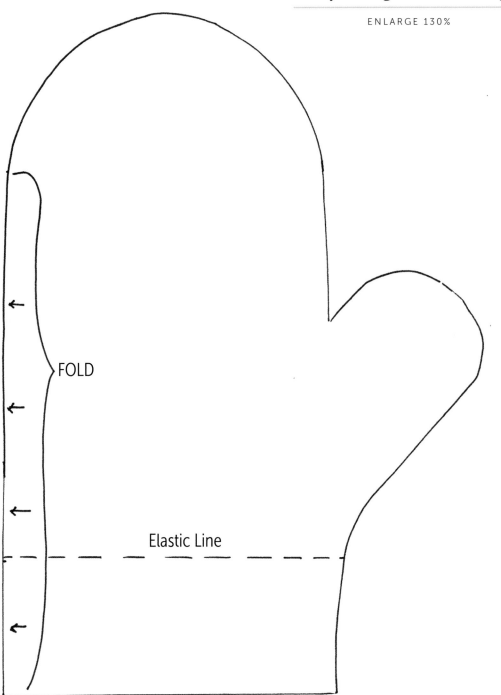

FOLD

Elastic Line

Monogram Pinboard

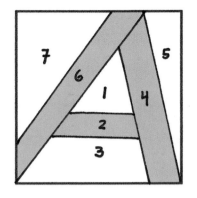
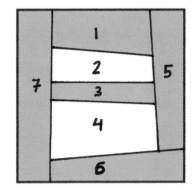
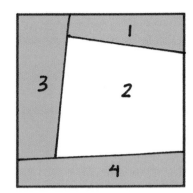

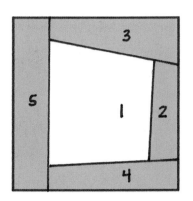
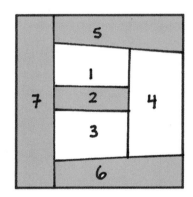
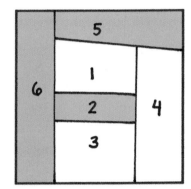

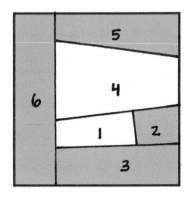
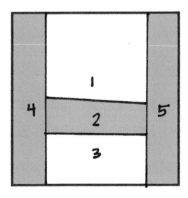
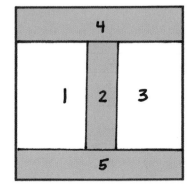

Monogram Pinboard

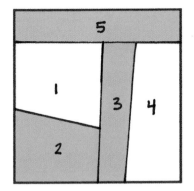

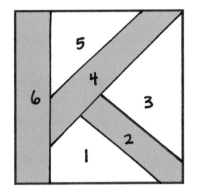

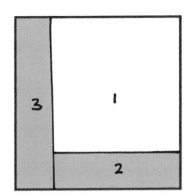

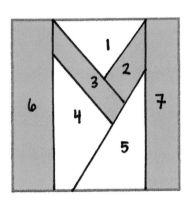

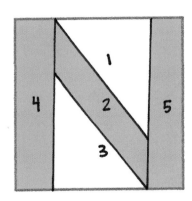

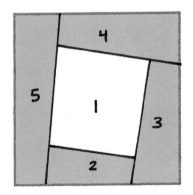

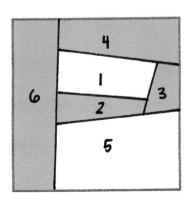

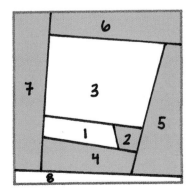

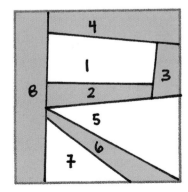

Monogram Pinboard

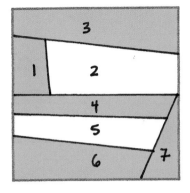

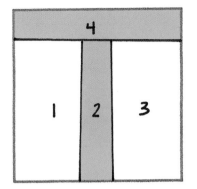

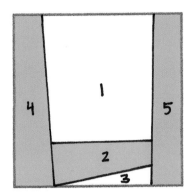

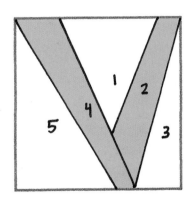

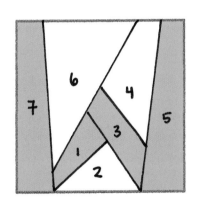

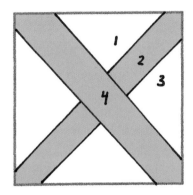

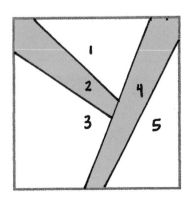

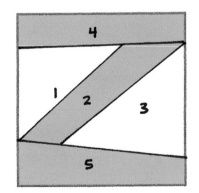

For the letter X:

Create a full block of sections 1, 2, and 3 as if section 4 is not there.

Then simply cut the block in half and sew piece 4 to both halves.

Wool House Slippers

Sole

Toe

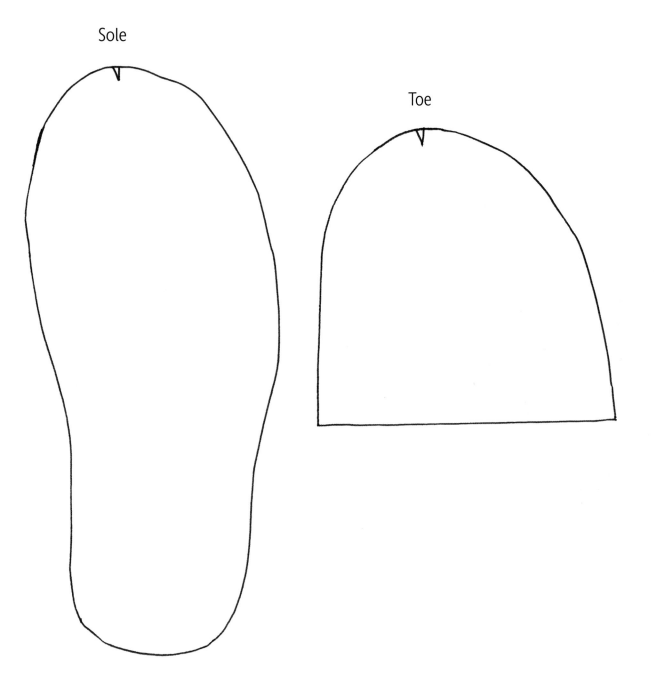

Acknowledgments

My heartfelt gratitude to all of the wonderful people who helped create this book.

Roost Books, for being a wonderful home and a pleasure to work with once again. Jennifer Urban-Brown, my editor, for wise insights about turning this book on its heels and gentle guidance along the way. Designer Colleen Cole and assistant editor Julia Gaviria for all your help.

Linda Roghaar, my agent, for sharing my enthusiasm for this project, as well as stories of personal heirlooms dear to your heart.

Morehouse Farm, for kind support and generously providing my favorite merino wool yarn used in a few projects in this book.

Cathy and all the lovely folks at The Artful Yarn in Chagrin Falls, for support and encouragement.

Kate, Sean, and Jen Tobin, for being such adorable and cheery models on a rainy morning down by the lake.

Beth, Desirée, Juliana, Julie, Jen, Sarah/Ida, and all my girlfriends for keeping me laughing.

My family—the one I was born into and the one I married into—for teaching me to value our heritage and traditions.

My daughters, Sophia + Natalie, for being who you are. What a delight it is to know you both!

And my husband, Patrick, for wisdom and thoughtful insights throughout our lifetime together.

Stitch Guide

Following are illustrated tutorials of basic hand-sewing and hand-embroidery techniques you may find useful when creating your own handmade heirlooms.

Basic Backstitch

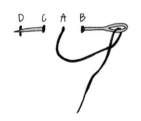

This is a great stitch for outlining and lettering. Working from right to left, bring the needle and thread up from back to front through A, down from front to back through B, up from back to front through C, down from front to back through A, up from back to front through D, and so on.

Blanket Stitch

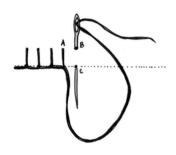

The blanket stitch is a popular method used for finishing the edges of fabrics. Working from left to right on the edge of the fabric, bring your needle and thread up from back to front through A ¼" from the edge of the fabric. Anchor the stitch by looping it over the edge and bringing it from back to front through A again. Insert the needle front to back through B to C, ¼" to the side of A, which is in the air at the edge of the fabric. Be sure to place the needle through the loop at the edge. Pull the stitch tight, aligning it with the edge of the fabric. Continue working stitches in this manner at ¼" intervals along the edge of the fabric.

Blind Stitch

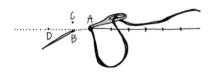

The blind stitch is a hidden stitch that is used for finishing quilts, hems, and anything where you do not wish the stitches to be seen. Working from right to left, bring the needle and thread from the front down through A, running it ¼" through the channel of the turned edge, then bring it up through B. Pick up a few strands of the opposite fabric, then bring the needle and thread from the front down C through D and continue working at ¼" intervals in this manner.

French Knot

French knots are ball-like knots that look terrific in many different types of embroidered projects. Bring the needle and thread up from back to front through A, hold the thread taut in one hand, and wrap the thread around the needle two times. Pull the thread so that the wraps are tight around the needle and then bring the needle and thread down from front to back near A (while still holding the thread taut around the needle).

Running Stitch

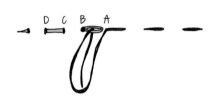

The running stitch creates a line of dashed stitches, which adds texture and gives an old-timey feel to embroidery. Bring the needle and thread up from back to front through A, down from front to back through B, up from back to front through C, down from front to back through D, and so on.

Knitting and Crochet Abbreviations + Tutorials

The projects in this book assume a general knowledge of knitting and crochet techniques. Following is an alphabetized list of abbreviations that are used throughout this book. For the more involved techniques, a written tutorial is provided alongside the definition. If you find that you need further instructions with visuals, check out the wonderful resources online with illustrations and videos of how to execute each of these stitches. For example, even though I have been knitting for nearly thirty years (oh my!), I only recently learned to crochet by watching tutorial videos on YouTube. So rather than offer overly wordy explanations, I suggest you look online if you need more involved tutorials. Many how-to videos are available, and I am certain you will be able to find some suited to your learning style.

3-Needle Bind Off

This smart-looking bind-off method using three needles is a really quick way to create a neat seam while binding off.

1. Place the stitches to bind off onto two needles and hold the knitting with the right sides together.

2. Place a third needle into the first stitch on the front needle as if to knit and again through the first stitch on the back needle as if to knit; then, knit those two stitches together.

3. Repeat this process for the next stitch on the front and back needles.

4. Use the left needle to pass the first stitch on the right needle over the second stitch and slide it off the right needle as you would with a traditional bind off.

5. Repeat this for the remaining stitches until one stitch remains on that third needle. You can then cut a tail of yarn and pull it through the loop to secure the last stitch.

Blocking   Blocking is a technique you do to finished knit pieces to smooth out the fabric and define the shape. Refer to the yarn manufacturer's care instructions to choose the best of these two blocking methods for your project.

- Steam blocking is the faster of the two methods, and it involves laying your knit piece flat on the ironing board and placing a light cloth on top to protect the piece. Hold the steam iron just above the surface to envelop it with steam. Set aside the iron and remove the cloth; then, use a ruler or measuring tape to shape the piece to the appropriate measurements. If needed, make another pass with the steam iron.

- Wet blocking involves literally wetting the finished piece. I like to soak it and then gently squeeze off excess water, while others prefer to use a spray bottle filled with water. Place the wet piece onto a padded surface (I use a blocking board). Then shape it to the appropriate measurements. You can use rust-proof pins to secure the shape where necessary.

- Always allow your finished pieces to dry completely before seaming.

BO   Bind off

C2B   Cable 2 to the back
This is a right-leaning two-stitch cable completed without using a cable needle.

1. Insert the right needle into the second stitch on the left needle from front to back as if to knit. Knit that stitch (one new stitch on the right needle now), but do not slip any stitches off the left needle yet.

2. Next, insert the right needle into the first stitch on the left needle as if to knit and knit it (now there are two new stitches on the right needle).

3. Finally, slip the first and second stitches off the left needle.

CH   Chain stitch

CO   Cast on

DC   Double crochet

dpns   Double pointed needles (typically sold in sets of five) are used for small works in the round.

Fat Quarter Yard   A full yard of fabric is cut once vertically and once horizontally into four equal pieces, each of which is commonly called a fat quarter.

Felting Knits in the Washing Machine   Wet the item(s) to be felted in a bucket filled with very hot water. When fully saturated, place the item(s) into a zippered pillowcase and close it securely. Fill the washing machine with hot water at the lowest water level and set the agitation at the fastest speed. Place the pillowcase into the washing machine along with a few pairs of old jeans or towels to help with agitation. Add a small amount (1 to 2 tablespoons) of detergent, dish soap, or baby shampoo. Turn on the washing machine and set a timer to be sure that it will not run through the spin cycle (that can cause unwanted folds in the finished piece). The amount of time it will take to felt will depend on the type of yarn used, the temperature and speed of the machine cycle, and the soap. Check in on it regularly and repeat the agitation cycle as needed. You will know it is done when the knitting is thick, dense, and smooth. Remove it from your machine and shape it with your hands. Allow the piece to dry completely, which may take a few days—you can set the piece on top of something (such as a cookie rack) to allow air to circulate underneath. Certain pieces need to be blocked for drying, while others are best left to dry on a form such as a box.

I-Cord
This knitted tube is made with three stitches and two double pointed needles. It looks great when used for ties and tassels and can be knotted to create woven fabric.

1. Cast on three stitches to a double pointed needle and knit those three stitches.

2. Do not turn the needle as if to purl; instead, slide the stitches to the other end of the needle and (without twisting) place the needle in your left hand.

3. Knit the three stitches again, pulling the yarn tightly so that it is snug when knitting that first stitch.

4. Repeat this process of knitting, sliding, and tugging until the I-Cord is the desired length.

5. To end, knit the three stitches together; then, cut a tail of yarn and pull it through the remaining the loop to secure the last stitch.

k
Knit the next stitch(es).

k2tog
Knit the next two stitches together; right-leaning decrease.

k2tog tbl
Knit the next two stitches together through the back loop; left-leaning decrease.

kfb
Knit into the front and back of the next stitch; single increase.

m1   Make one new stitch.

This is my preferred method of increasing without visible bumps or holes in the work.

1. Insert the left needle from front to back to lift the strand between the stitch just worked (on the right needle) and the stitch about to be worked (on the left needle).

2. Knit that stitch through the back loop.

p   Purl

PM   Place marker

PSSO   Pass the slipped stitch over the previously knitted stitch

PU   Pick up additional stitch(es)

Seed Stitch   When repeated over several rows, this simple stitch pattern creates a lovely dotted motif that is fully reversible.

1. On the right side of your work, do a repeat of (k1, p1) to the end of the row.

2. Then on the wrong side, purl the knit stitches and knit the purl stitches.

Sl   Slip the next stitch

SSK   Slip slip knit (slip the next two stitches knitwise, then slip the left needle through the fronts of them and knit them together)

st(s)   Stitch(es)

St st   Stockinette Stitch (knitting on the right side, purling on the wrong side)

w&t   Wrap and turn

This technique will prevent holes from forming when creating short rows (such as the ones created for the soles of the Ankle Booties [page 19]).

1. Bring the yarn to the front of your work (as if to purl) and then slip one stitch purlwise from the left needle to the right needle.

2. Turn your work, bring the yarn to the front, then slip that same stitch from the left needle to the right needle.

3. Work the wrap with the wrapped stitch together as you come to it in the next row.

wyib   With yarn in back (hold the yarn in the back of the work as if to knit)

wyif   With yarn in front (hold the yarn in the front of the work as if to purl)

Resources

Fabric + Notions

Cotton & Steel Fabrics • cottonandsteelfabrics.com

Custom Knits & Mfg. (blocking boards) • customknitsmfg.com

Fat Quarter Shop • fatquartershop.com

JoAnn Fabrics • joann.com

Purl Soho • purlsoho.com

Robert Kaufman Fabrics • robertkaufman.com

Sew, Mama, Sew • sewmamasew.com

Superbuzzy • superbuzzy.com

Wool Felt + Stuffing

A Child's Dream Come True • achildsdream.com

Craft Wool Felt • etsy.com/shop/CraftyWoolFelt

Filz Felt • filzfelt.com

Magic Cabin • magiccabin.com

Morehouse Farm Merino • morehousefarm.com

Purl Soho • purlsoho.com

Wool Felt Grab Bags • etsy.com/shop/WoolFeltGrabBags

Wool Yarns
(a few of my favorite worsted weight yarns
for knitting + felting)

Cascade 220 • cascadeyarns.com

Morehouse Merino 3-Strand Yarn • morehousefarm.com

Plymouth Galway Wool • plymouthyarn.com

Quince & Co. Lark • quinceandco.com

Stone Hedge Fiber Mill Shepherd's Wool • stonehedgefibermill.com

Books

Colton, Virginia, ed. *Complete Guide to Needlework* (Reader's Digest). White Plains, NY: Reader's Digest, 1979.

Cornell, Kari, ed. *Baby Knits from Around the World: Twenty Heirloom Projects in a Variety of Styles and Techniques.* Minneapolis: Creative Publishing International, 2013.

Corwin, Lena. *Lena Corwin's Made by Hand: A Collection of Projects to Print, Sew, Weave, Dye, Knit, or Otherwise Create.* New York: Stewart, Tabori and Chang, 2013.

Falick, Melanie, and Kristin Nicholas. *Knitting for Baby: 30 Heirloom Projects with Complete How-to-Knit Instructions.* New York: Stewart, Tabori and Chang, 2002.

Hoverson, Joelle. *Last-Minute Patchwork and Quilted Gifts.* New York: STC Craft, 2007.

Koseki, Suzuko. *Natural Patchwork: 26 Stylish Projects Inspired by Flowers, Fabric, and Home.* Boston: Roost Books, 2011.

Koseki, Suzuko. *Patchwork Style: 35 Simple Projects for a Cozy and Colorful Life.* Boston: Roost Books, 2009.

Mano, Akiko. *Linen, Wool, Cotton: 25 Simple Projects to Sew with Natural Fabrics.* Boston: Roost Books, 2009.

Martin, Tovah. *Tasha Tudor's Heirloom Crafts.* Boston and New York: Houghton Mifflin Co., 1995.

Morey, Carrie. *Callie's Biscuits and Southern Traditions: Heirloom Recipes from Our Family Kitchen.* New York: Atria Books, 2013.

Paulson, Alicia. *Embroidery Companion: Classic Designs for Modern Living.* New York: Potter Craft, 2010.

Ridge, Brent, and Josh Kilmer-Purcell. *The Beekman 1802 Heirloom Cookbook.* New York: Sterling Epicure, 2011.

Soule, Amanda. *Handmade Home: Simple Ways to Repurpose Old Materials into New Family Treasures.* Boston: Roost Books, 2009.

Stocker, Blair. *WiseCraft: Turning Thrift Store Finds, Fabric Scraps, and Natural Objects into Stuff You Love.* Philadelphia: Running Press, 2014.

Sutcliffe, Kristen. *Fabric Paper Thread: 26 Projects to Sew & Embellish 25 Embroidery Stitches.* Concord, CA: C&T Publishing, 2013.

Periodicals

Better Homes and Gardens

Cotton Friend (Japan)

Cotton Time (Japan)

Country Living

Flea Market Style

Home Sweet Craft (Japan)

Make It Vintage

Martha Stewart Living

Mollie Makes (UK)

Stitch

Taproot

Websites + Craft Blogs

Dottie Angel (Tif Fussell)—dottieangel.blogspot.com

Elise Blaha Cripe—eliseblaha.typepad.com

Erleperle (Mette Robl)—mette-erleperle.blogspot.com

Flax and Twine (Anne Weil)—flaxandtwine.com

Fons and Porter—fonsandporter.com

Friedas Retro GalERIE—friedafliegenpilz.blogspot.com

Gretelies—gretelies.blogspot.com

The Heirloom Project—theheirloomproject.co.uk

Hildas Hem—hildashem.se

Hodge Podge Farm (Cal Patch)—hodgepodgefarm.net

House on Hill Road (Erin Harris)—houseonhillroad.com

The Long Thread (Ellen Luckette Baker)—thelongthread.com

Lotta Jansdotter—jansdotter.com

Meet Me at Mikes (Pip Lincolne)—meetmeatmikes.com

Miko Design—mikodesign.blogspot.com

Noodlehead (Anna Graham)—noodle-head.com

Petits Details—petitsdetails.com

Small Forest (Wendy Hill)—smallforestshop.blogspot.com

Smile and Wave (Rachel Denbow)—smileandwave.typepad.com

Soulemama (Amanda Soule)—soulemama.com

Sparkle Power (Candace Todd)—sparklepower.etsy.com

Squam Art Workshops—squamartworkshops.com

Wisecraft (Blair Stocker)—wisecrafthandmade.com

About the Author

Jennifer Casa is a maker of modern heirlooms. She sews, knits, and combines new + vintage materials to create unique handmade pieces with the intention that they to be used and treasured for generations. She has written several books including *Vintage Made Modern: Transforming Timeworn Textiles into Treasured Heirlooms* (Roost Books 2014). She lives in northern Ohio with her husband and twin daughters.

Connect with her at JCasahandmade.com.